Praise f[or]
The Light is W[inning]

By all accounts, Zach Hoag should be a "done" who has given up on the church and a hard-bitten cynic turning his back on Christianity. But he's not. Surviving a childhood in an apocalyptic cult and the deep disappointment of a failed church as a young adult, Zach Hoag has pressed on to find a mature, authentic, and sustainable faith. Beyond doom and gloom eschatology and overwrought revivalism, there is a place of healthy religion where the light is winning. Zach Hoag is a faithful guide to this better place, and I hope many a wounded and disappointed soul will follow him there.

—**Brian Zahnd**, lead pastor of Word of Life Church in St. Joseph, Missouri, and the author of several books, including *Sinners in the Hands of a Loving God*, *Water to Wine*, and *A Farewell to Mars*

When I survey twenty-first century America, I fight to avoid depression and despair. But in such a moment, Zach Hoag has swept in with a prophetic message bursting with optimism. The darkness is real, he admits, but it is also receding. Hoag refocuses our collective gaze and argues convincingly that America is entering a time of "Great Revealing." So sit back and read slowly. *The Light Is Winning* pulls back the cultural curtain to reveal not a wizard, but a blinding light of hope.

—**Jonathan Merritt**, contributing writer for *The Atlantic* and author of *Learning to Speak God from Scratch*

So often authors write about their successes. What I love about Zach is he's given us a rare and precious opportunity to witness his apparent defeat, allowing us to watch as he wrestles with his upbringing in an authoritarian cult and his subsequent journey through denominations and church planting. Zach uses his stories to invite us into some deeper truths about the church today, offering hope during a tumultuous time in American Christianity. And maybe the best part of all of this? He draws inspiration from TV shows, like *Breaking Bad* and *The Walking Dead*. When someone tells me we don't want an undead zombie faith, I find myself nodding along.

–**Melanie Dale**, author of *It's Not Fair*
and *Women Are Scary*

In his hopeful new book, *The Light Is Winning*, Zach reminds us that while deconstructing our religious faith might be a necessary part of our spiritual journey, it's not enough. Zach encourages us to rebuild a proper religious practice, one that demonstrates the power and mystery of Christianity: the resurrection.

–**Elizabeth Esther**, author of
Girl at the End of the World

Zach Hoag writes with a deep love for the church and a tender pastor's heart. He has known loss and pain, but most importantly, he has turned to the light in the midst of darkness, and the hope he writes about is what we all desperately need today.

–**Ed Cyzewski**, author of *A Christian Survival Guide* and *Coffeehouse Theology*

I needed to read this book. As somebody who has long been disillusioned by religion and tempted to give up on the church, *The Light Is Winning* was a much-needed dose of hope for me. I found my own perspectives being challenged not only by Hoag's thoughts and ideas about God and culture but also by his beautiful story and the cheerful and endearing way in which he tells it.

–Matthew Paul Turner, author of *Churched*
and *When God Made You*

Zach Hoag's personal and ecclesiastic apocalypse will draw you into his story and perhaps your own moment of revealing. You will cheer when you realize, like him, that the light is indeed winning!

–Kelley Nikondeha, codirector, Communities
of Hope and author, *Adopted: The Sacrament
of Belonging in a Fractured World*

Only Zach Hoag could bring out the hope in an apocalypse. Leading us toward the light of authentic religion at the end of the post-modern tunnel we call being "spiritual", *The Light Is Winning* is the kind of book that you will want to keep on your nightstand for months, maybe years. You will want to reach for it each time you begin to lose your way and your faith.

–Jerusalem Jackson Greer, author
of *At Home in this Life*

Zach takes the reader on a journey, first acknowledging the presence of these religious wounds, then gently leading us through a hopeful apocalypse to a place of transformation and healing.

–Shawn Smucker, author and writer

We live in a world that often seems overcome with darkness and pessimism. Between toxic news cycles, Christian in-fighting, and what feels like a nonstop dose of negativity on all sides, people are left longing for a message of hope—I am left longing for a message of hope. I am grateful for this book, because while I don't pretend to have answers for the darkened world around us, I do know this: the world needs to know that the light is winning.

—Benjamin L. Corey, author of *Unafraid: Moving Beyond Fear-Based Faith*

The Light Is
Winning

The Light Is Winning

Why Religion Just Might

Bring Us Back to Life

Zach Hoag

 ZONDERVAN®

ZONDERVAN

The Light Is Winning
Copyright © 2017 by Zach Hoag

Requests for information should be addressed to:
Zondervan, *3900 Sparks Dr. SE, Grand Rapids, Michigan 49546*

ISBN 978-0-310-34786-6 (softcover)

ISBN 978-0-310-35052-1 (audio)

ISBN 978-0-310-34821-4 (ebook)

Published in association with literary agent Jenni Burke of D.C. Jacobson and
Associates LLC, an Author Management Company. www.dcjacobson.com

Some of the names and locations in this book have been changed to protect
individuals' privacy.

Cover design: Curt Diepenhorst
Interior design: Kait Lamphere

First printing April 2017 / Printed in the United States of America

Contents

Part I

Illusion and Revelation

Chapter 1

Apocalypse Now

The worst things often begin with the best intentions. Like that time my family moved to a Texas cult.

I had just reached the age of accountability when we loaded up the family sedan and set off from the sweltering concrete suburbs of Miami for the orange clay fields of a little town called Jasper. I had no idea what a cult is, much less that we were moving to one. I just knew we were on a mission from God. We might as well have been leaving Harran for the land of Canaan like Father Abraham, destined for "the city with foundations, whose architect and builder is God."*

My father was a radical man, drawn to radical men. That's why he and my mother, along with a faithful remnant from the church they had planted in Miami years earlier, decided to uproot. As the earnest eldest son, my indoctrination was total; I was all in. It wouldn't be the least bit difficult to forget the worldly friends and relatives we were leaving behind. They just didn't get it, and neither did the rest of the lukewarm American church.

We were the ones who were on fire for Jesus. We were the

---

* Hebrews 11:10.

ones willing to forsake all and follow him, to ditch the trappings of easy, dead religion for the harder, wilder road of Spirit-filled discipleship. Discipleship—that was the key word in those days. Were you willing to give up everything—all your money, all your relationships, all your time and energy, all your goals—to learn from the divinely ordained, end-times apostles and prophets? In the tiny town of Jasper, Texas, there was the School of the Prophets, a superspiritual sort of Bible college waiting for my father and his Floridian followers. There they would finally rise above the ordinary class of believer and learn from the anointed leaders God had put in place for the perilous last days. Perilous last days—a fitting description of the late 1980s, really.

There was much joy and laughter and unity in the beginning. Our group arrived in waves of Ryder trucks and compact cars, a sprawling modern-day caravan of bedouins migrating to our new Promised Land. Those early shared dinners and church services were electric, as our Miami community excitedly integrated itself with this new Jasper community, all while maintaining our strong ties. We were getting the lay of the land together, urban explorers in a new rural territory, anchored by the church compound and its magnetic, mystical quality. Perhaps our group even exceeded the local members in our singular devotion and irrepressible energy. We had left everything behind, because none of it could ever measure up to the power and revelation emanating from this one church, this one spot on the globe. We were in on the ground floor of something truly life- and world-changing. And we were in it together.

There's a home video of me on one of those early days in Texas, before our rental was ready for us to move into. I am in the orange-dappled front yard of the house where we are staying, and church bells are ringing in the distance. I have a toy gun, the kind that makes an automatic firing sound, and I am holding down the trigger all the way, growling like Rambo, "Let me at that Babylonian church!"

I too am a radical, a militant, at ten years old.

●   ●   ●

"I'll fly away, oh glory, I'll fly away—in the morning!"

In a large field on the compound, I joined a group of friends from the church school for a hay ride. It was fall, and we reached for hoodies and blankets to fight the nighttime chill. The older kids led the song, one that I'd never heard before, having been raised in a church born in the aftermath of the charismatic Jesus Movement of the 1970s. We proudly stood in the hippie tradition of bucking tradition, preferring '80s Christian rock and kickdancing near the altar to classic hymns or organ music.

It didn't matter much because the older kids were singing the song ironically: at the church in East Texas, we didn't believe in flying away. We didn't believe in the rapture. The doctrine taught by Brother Dawson and the elders was part of the Latter Rain or Manifest Sons of God school of thought. We believed in a progressive manifestation of the kingdom of God in the last days through divinely appointed apostles and prophets. In the midst of troubled times for everyone else, the true church would experience unprecedented levels of spiritual power with many signs and wonders ushering in a great revival and widespread dominion in the days leading up to the second coming of Christ.

Brother Dawson was one such apostle and prophet. (He claimed both titles.) A former regular on Christian TV who had been exiled for misbehavior, he had both the popularity and the rebel edge befitting a charismatic end-times guru. People just like us from all over the country had descended on this tiny East Texas town to learn from him, drawn primarily by his teaching tape ministry and his one published book. My father had become a disciple of Brother Dawson's long before in Miami; he disappeared into his bedroom to devour every puffy case of audio or video tapes that arrived in the mail, filling stacks of spiral-bound notebooks with scrawled notes. These teachings were for him a source of unparalleled revelation from God. When we arrived in Jasper, he enrolled in the School of the Prophets to get the training necessary to be numbered among the Manifest Sons of God and, perhaps more important, among the inner circle of Brother Dawson's elders.

Despite this somewhat novel view of the last days, the urgency of the end surrounded everything we did at the church. It was the secret of the church's success. The multibuilding compound became the hub of my life, a perpetual-motion machine of school and worship services and home group meetings. Many of the worship services were called on unscheduled weeknights by the elders, seemingly on a whim, with mandatory attendance. The schedule for home group meetings was constantly changing or stopping or restarting to coincide with the elders' latest instructions, corrections, and revelations for the congregation. Brother Dawson often directed everything from the seclusion of his enormous ranch on the other side of town, disappearing for weeks to seek out the next series of visions and messages while being served by women, whom he called his handmaidens, handpicked from the congregation. In all of this motion, obligation, and orchestration, we were inundated by urgency: the prophet of

God possessed the word of the Lord for this desperate hour, and our adherence to it would make the difference between eternal life and lukewarm death when the end came.

And for all I knew, the end was coming soon, and very soon.

A Great Revealing

As a militant ten-year-old in Jasper, Texas, I could not have foreseen any future in which the Manifest Sons of God were not on the move, releasing revelation, working miracles, sparking revival, and exercising dominion. I wanted to be among them, living out a call to ministry that had gripped me back in Miami: to walk in all the powerful potential of an end-times apostle or prophet.

I certainly could not have foreseen the future that awaited me: one of rejecting the end-times doctrine of my youth and ending up a thirty-three-year-old failed church-planter in the least religious state in the US. I couldn't have anticipated the cultural shift that would take place at that time—a shift not toward greater power and dominion for the church but toward an increasingly post-Christian reality.

Not in a million years.

That American Christianity is in significant decline is no longer news. The numbers, at least, are undeniable: all streams of Christianity in the US—Roman Catholic, Eastern Orthodox, mainline Protestant, and evangelical—are shrinking as a share or percentage of the US population. And the rate of the decline has only accelerated since the turn of the century.[1]

At the same time, the share of those who practice non-Christian faiths or who claim no religious affiliation is on the rise. The latter group has been referred to colloquially as "the nones" because they check the "none" box when asked to name their religious affiliation. In a groundbreaking study, the Pew Research Forum has tracked this rise from less than 15 percent of the population in the early aughts to nearly a quarter of the population now, and it's still climbing.[2] (For reference, in 1972 the percentage of folks checking that none box was in the single digits.)[3] The share of people practicing non-Christian religions has also risen.

And we see this trend in our communities, don't we? Kids from the youth group go off to college and disengage from church; friends and family lose interest in things related to faith or find church attendance irrelevant, if not impossible to work into their schedules; we have doubts about whether church makes sense or adds anything to our lives. All of us are caught up in a current that seems to be pulling us away from Christian faith, not toward it.

Despite the external stability of some Christian churches, denominations, or groups, the dramatic rise of the religiously unaffiliated signals a stark generational shift, with millennials and other young adults in the rising majority of the nones. Fewer millennials (around 27 percent) attend religious services than any other demographic group.[4] And the nones themselves are also becoming more secular.[5] To put this into perspective, author and journalist Jonathan Merritt warns all Christian groups against taking comfort in momentarily placing toward the top of a "race to the bottom."[6] And no single category (like conservative or progressive) can be directly linked to increase or decrease, as all kinds of denominations and movements have experienced this decline.

We are at least witnessing an overall trend toward pluralism (religious diversity) and secularism (religious nonadherence) similar to what other Western countries have already experienced. A post-Christian[7] cultural reality is setting in, and in many areas of the country, such as where I live in New England, it is already well entrenched.

But there is something unique about the American trend because of the central role Christianity has played in our nation's history. This decline is being felt by Christians of all stripes—and perhaps especially by evangelicals and mainline Protestants—as a deep and lamentable loss. A loss of culture, a loss of tradition, a loss of institutions, a loss of influence.

And with each denominational downsizing, church closure, and failed startup attempt, the picture becomes a little more grim. Many of the faithful fail to see anything good or hopeful about it. Some prominent Christians view this at best as an encroaching period of exile for the church[8] or at worst as an escalating collapse.[9]

But I prefer to view it as something else.

I see it as an apocalypse.

●   ●   ●

I know what you're thinking. What could blood moons, the rapture, and the end of the world possibly have to do with the decline of Christian faith in the US? Is this trend in church attendance signaling the end of days?

No area of Christian theology is more intriguing to the popular imagination than the end times, especially fearful predictions of the great tribulation playing out on the world stage. The bestselling Left Behind series has become a full-length movie franchise, an HBO series chronicles the lives of *The Leftovers*, and the rapture has even formed the backdrop of a James Franco and Seth Rogen buddy comedy. Whenever a lunar eclipse approaches on the calendar, blood moon evangelists make the viral video rotation on Facebook. And the zombie apocalypse has never been more popular, with numerous films and television series representing its grim and grotesque vision of great tribulation.

While in that Texas cult we roundly rejected the rapture as an escapist fantasy of the worldly Babylonian church, we expected the great tribulation, which would, along with the great revival, lead us to the end. We were thoroughly apocalyptic in our orientation, fixated on the full stop to human history that was coming soon, and very soon.

But we, like so many people, misunderstood what the word apocalypse means. We were misguided in our association of the apocalyptic Scriptures with the end of human history.

The primary biblical source for all things end times is, of course, the book of Revelation. The book's name comes from the first verse of the first chapter, where the apostle John writes, "The revelation from Jesus Christ, which God gave him to show his servants what must soon take place." The Greek word for revelation here is *apokalypsis*. Apocalypse!

For this reason, some traditions even call the book the Apocalypse of John.

According to New Testament scholar Michael Gorman, the word apocalypse "does not mean 'destruction,' 'end of the world,' or anything similar."[10] *Apocalypse* literally means "revealing." It means "unveiling" or "disclosure." And John's apocalypse is revealing much more than information about the end of human history. Here's Gorman again: "Revelation is (primarily) good news about Christ, the Lamb of God—who shares God's throne and who is the key to the past, present, and future—and therefore also about uncompromising faithfulness leading to undying hope, even in the midst of unrelenting evil and oppressive empire."[11]

While the final hope of the world is certainly an important part of John's strange and powerful letter, it is not a roadmap to the end times. There are no coded geopolitical events and cataclysmic cultural timelines to be uncovered, no raptures or blood moons (not to mention beasts, battles of Armageddon, or foreheads tattooed 666). Instead, there is a pattern that applies first to the believers in John's time, which is why the apostle says these insights "must soon take place" for his original readers. And that pattern applies second to believers throughout all time, giving us a template for what worshiping and following Jesus, the Lamb who is King, mean at personal, cultural, and even political levels.

This apocalyptic pattern always deals with ends and beginnings, anticipating the final end and the new age that begins thereafter. For John's original readers, an ending indeed was taking place. You might say his apocalypse was a great revealing anticipating a necessary ending for the church in his day, one brought about both by intensifying oppression and persecution from the empire, and by compromise and failure in the churches themselves. And that ending was leading to a brilliant new beginning, when the church would revive, root down, and find true flourishing.

The sharp decline we are witnessing today invites all kinds of reactions, from denial to ambivalence to acquiescence to outright panic. But if we take a cue from Scripture, and particularly Revelation, and view this decline through the lens of apocalypse, we might have a different reaction altogether.

We might see an opportunity to reflect on what is being revealed, embrace the change that is needed, and move forward in newness of life. After all, isn't that how the story goes? Life to death, death to resurrection.

After the Apocalypse

Perhaps the connection I'm making between apocalypse and the decline of Christianity in the US seems grandiose. That's understandable. But what I'm doing, at the basic level, is making a suggestion and an observation. First, I'm suggesting that whenever the church faces significant difficulty, decline, or suffering, it is an opportunity for churchwide reflection that might lead to reformation, and the biblical vision of apocalypse helps us to frame this. Second, I'm observing trends and events not from a distance but from the front lines of various segments of the American church, including my experiences planting a church in a thoroughly post-Christian part of the country (New England).

But perhaps that doesn't go deep enough either.

Because really, this book is a story.

The story of my apocalypse. And no matter what, it's the story of what happens—what has to happen—after the apocalypse.

In 2008, when we were only in our late twenties, my wife and I decided to plant a church. I had long abandoned the cultish experience of my youth and was making every effort to forge ahead in faith and life. I had a great job in the snowboard industry, was happily married, and had most recently served in youth group and small group ministry at a relatively stable and successful Baptist church. But Kalen and I wanted to venture into this new work because we shared a conviction, based on our experiences in both career and ministry, that there was a heartbreaking gap between the churches in our area and the non-Christian friends whom we loved. We lived in what was then the least religious state in the nation (Vermont), right next door to the least religious city in that state (Burlington), a place where the decline of Christianity had long ago taken root and a secular, post-Christian culture was well established. We desperately wanted our friends to know Jesus, and we didn't feel comfortable inviting them to any of the churches we attended or ministered in.

And that's because we knew something was wrong with the church in our place. We felt that wrongness perhaps most palpably when it came to our attempts at evangelism. It all led to the same dead end.

What we felt was the urgency of the decline all around us, even though we wouldn't have put it in those words at the time. The nonreligiousness of our place was not a statistical theory but a lived reality, and we sensed that the apparent stability of that Baptist church masked the missional crisis at hand. The nones outside the church walls were only growing in number, and it felt like entire generational and cultural groups were being left out or even shut out. Starting a new church seemed like the right solution, maybe the only solution, to our dilemma, and the Spirit seemed to be leading us in that direction almost effortlessly, inexorably.

But perhaps I should have known that the worst things often begin with the best intentions.

* * *

The 1979 film *Apocalypse Now* begins with the protagonist, Captain Benjamin Willard, played by Martin Sheen, holed up in a hotel room somewhere in Vietnam. He's waiting to be sent back into the battlefield. He's waiting for a mission: "Everyone gets everything he wants. I wanted a mission, and for my sins, they gave me one. Brought it up to me like room service. It was a real choice mission, and when it was over, I never wanted another."[12]

I was just a little pastor's kid when I first caught the bug. I experienced early what Christians refer to as a call to ministry. Surely this was facilitated and reinforced by my church and family environments. But I also felt and believed in this call at the deepest level of my little being. This call matured into an earnest militancy at ten, and it helped me survive all the ministry drama and trauma of my childhood and adolescence, becoming an anchor amid ever-increasing storms of confusion. As a young adult, even after everything I grew up around, I still wanted a mission, a mission from God, in a real, sincere, abiding way. I couldn't shake it.

But when my own church plant came crashing to an end in late 2012, I was sure that I'd never want another.

Maybe this is the story of your apocalypse too, illuminating the moment of great revealing that brought your life of faith, or your church and ministry dreams, to a sudden and unexpected end.

Maybe you've been hurt or abused by the church. Or maybe you're just worn out, exhausted by the effort to perpetuate the institution. Maybe you've looked behind the curtain of ministry and found disappointment at best or phony props at worst. Maybe you've put idealism and hope and certainty into a ministry project that came up terribly short or, worse, failed spectacularly. Maybe you've worked for years to be an agent of change within your church or movement only to hit roadblock after dream-crushing roadblock. Maybe it's the church community that has marginalized and excluded you, while those outside the church have loved and accepted you.

Maybe you're one of those people—young or old—who are just done with church, even though they love Jesus and are holding on to their faith.

And maybe you just don't see the point. Maybe you're one of the nones who are diligently spiritual, but checking the box—and keeping up the commitments—of organized religion confines and kills the vibrancy of their spiritual experience. Maybe you're drawn to Jesus, but the church makes no sense. Especially the church's hypocrisy and brokenness, which seem to be plastered across your newsfeed every day.

If any of this describes you, consider that all of our stories might be caught up in a bigger story. Not just the story of the decline of Christian faith in America but the story of a transition in which ineffective, harmful, and toxic things are being revealed and brought to a necessary end. A story in which that ending leads to a brilliant new beginning, just like it always has in the church's story—death paving the way for a resurrected, rooted, flourishing faith, opening the door into an abiding hope and a bright future.

After the apocalypse.

Chapter 2

Beyond the Numbers

The issues we've been looking at are not new. The apostle John begins his book of prophetic Revelation by revealing the state of the churches in his day (chapters 1–2), identifying the compromises and failures (and some successes) relevant to the end that was upon them. I think this provides a model for us in looking at our moment of decline.

Judgment, the apostle said, begins with God's household,* and it is indeed a great revealing. The question is what exactly is being revealed.

Perhaps the best place to begin is with my personal end. When we closed our church in 2012, my life was enveloped by a haze. All of the ministry and community ideals I'd held so tightly were in disarray. Around that time, I attended a conference about church revitalization. It was a strange experience. I was still so beat up and broken, so uncertain about my future in ministry or even church.

I found myself in a breakout session led by a Canadian missiologist. As the speaker talked, I was drawn in because what he

---

* 1 Peter 4:17.

was saying cut against the grain of problem-solution thinking, which I was so weary of. A failed church-planter who is not in denial doesn't give a rip about the latest models for turning a small, declining church or organization into an exponentially larger, more influential, and more successful one, because you've learned that so few of those models bear any resemblance to reality. Some of them are downright illusions.

It seemed to me that this missiologist had learned that too. Everything he was saying felt like a breath of fresh air.

So when the time seemed right (when it was most awkward), I blurted out a question: "What do you think of all the studies and theories about how to get millennials and the nones and everyone else back to church?"

He replied, "It's all BS!"

The speaker's honesty ignited a strange hope within me. What I think he meant is that so much of the conversation about the statistics hovers above solutions and strategies rather than going deep to reveal root issues. It is not, as I've said, that the numbers are wrong; it's that the discussions about them are flawed, exercises in willful ignorance often skewed toward replenishing institutions and organizations rather than accomplishing a deeper and more durable mission. The missiologist suggested that when we push past the BS, we might see root issues like rampant individualism and laissez-faire capitalism, an underlying cultural paradigm that the American church has swallowed hook, line, and sinker.

It was not your typical Christian conference fodder, that's for sure.

●   ●   ●

Another missiologist has pointed out similar issues in his book *The End of Evangelicalism?* This author, David Fitch, looks to atheist political philosopher Slavoj Zizek for a psychoanalysis of American Christianity in decline. And what he finds is that Christians have often succumbed to *ideology*—"a big lie with which we can all cooperate in order to keep our lives going."[1] He identifies how ideology plays out in basic beliefs and practices that define our Christian group identity but become empty or even harmful. These empty beliefs and practices "have allowed us to consent to what we know is a lie," a kind of willful ignorance that refuses to look at the deeper truths boiling beneath the surface, what Zizek calls "the Real."[2]

I believe this moment of great revealing is leading us, first and foremost, to the real.

If we see the current shift to a post-Christian culture as an apocalypse—a revealing—then we can look for what is being revealed instead of bemoaning the losses. We might see that the realities of the kingdom of God have too often been hidden beneath our ideologies, the ideals and illusions of our own making.

Take the common desire among American Christians to be *relevant* as a reaction to the decline. When I was a church planter, I believed that my skinny jeans and American Apparel hoodie (it was the aughts, people) would at least be *helpful* in starting a truly missional church community. And our indie-folk worship band, which wrote rousing tunes that could just as easily be played in a club as in a Sunday service, couldn't hurt either, right? Even more, our graphic design was always on point, and it's just a verifiable fact that we had the best church website in 2009. We placed a lot of stock in our relevance, especially in the first years of our journey. But this relevance couldn't sustain us. It couldn't prevent the inevitable failures we faced.

I'm not trying to be cynical. And I realize that you may already be asking yourself whether there's any hope for the American church. This take on the numbers and our often flawed reactions to them may come off as so pessimistic.

Or maybe you feel like things are just fine with your faith and your church, thank you very much. Maybe you're part of one of those church communities that really is relevant and has led to some good things.

But this is why the apocalyptic perspective is so needed. It helps us see beyond both the statistical decline and the surface successes. It points us to the deeper level—the level of kingdom reality, the realest of the real. And it communicates that the decline of Christian faith in America is not a problem to be solved but an opportunity to be embraced. I trust that you are reading this because, like me, you want to embrace that opportunity too. Or maybe you at least want to hope that such an opportunity exists.

But not everyone is looking for this opportunity, and not everyone will embrace it. Some will continue to uphold the status quo at all costs, and some will be successful in doing so, at least for a time.

To participate in this apocalyptic revealing and ultimately get to the real, we must heed the words of the apostle: "Today, if you hear his voice, do not harden your hearts"*—because the BS happens when we don't face the root issues but instead seek temporary solutions to perpetuate what is already passing away,

---

* Hebrews 3:7–8.

when we miss the forest fire among the trees that haven't yet been set ablaze, and when we choose our ideals and illusions, even if they are as innocent as a desire for relevance and cultural coolness, over deeper kingdom realities.

Really, this apocalypse transcends the statistics of decline. It's an *eruption of the real*.[3] It's an opportunity to glimpse what's underneath the surface of American Christianity and even our own faith, and then to seek healing, reformation, and progress.

Because it's when we courageously face the real, despite how difficult and painful it may be, that we can move beyond ideology and find a flourishing faith.

Enter: Empire

The name Walter White has been etched into our collective American consciousness. The protagonist of the award-winning AMC series *Breaking Bad* is nothing less than a cultural icon, his status secured by digital binge-watchers and old-school DVD collectors alike. His legend even lives on in a prequel spinoff series centered on Walter's sketchy lawyer, Saul Goodman. *Breaking Bad's* narrative virtually defines an era we now call the new golden age of television, perfecting the art of the dark antihero in a desperate downward spiral.

Walter White is an underpaid high school chemistry teacher who has terminal cancer and decides to cook and sell crystal meth to leave behind a nest egg for his family. But in the process, he "breaks bad." This once mild-mannered husband and father develops startling levels of brutality as he morphs into the fearsome drug kingpin Heisenberg.

Walt's downward spiral is epic because he starts out on such solid ground. He is just a regular guy, a good citizen, a respected neighbor—as any one of us might envision ourselves. Yet with each decision, he descends farther, and we are invited to imagine ourselves descending with him.

If the show has a moral, it would be that given the right amount of pressure and pain, every one of us is capable of breaking bad. We have a choice in each trying moment. Will we surrender or seize control? Will we break good or break bad?[4]

In one particularly powerful moment in the show's farewell season, Walt's weary protege Jesse arrives at his door. Jesse is distraught, guilt ridden after the carnage inflicted by their joint criminal operation. He implores Walter to sell the meth business to another cartel and be done with it. This is Walt's chilling reply: "Jesse, you asked me if I was in the meth business or the money business. Neither. I'm in the *empire* business."[5]

While the word empire might conjure different images for different people—including, I'm sure, scenes from the Star Wars franchise—we can define it simply as "the sinful human system of selfish power and control." When sinful people on a large scale seek selfish power and control over people, places, and circumstances, empire is the result. And because empire is an ocean we're all swimming in, the system seeps into each of us in such a way that we may, at any time and in a multitude of ways, get caught up in empire business.

Some of us may even find ourselves breaking bad.

It hasn't yet been developed into a prestige TV drama, but a startling encounter recorded in three of the four gospels communicates something similarly important about empire. A woman approaches Jesus while he is dining at the house of Simon the leper. She is carrying a jar of expensive perfume or ointment, which she breaks and pours over Jesus' head so that the perfume runs all over his body. While visions of the Super Bowl Gatorade ritual immediately come to mind, there is something more somber about this sacrament. Mark's account has Jesus clarifying, "She poured perfume on my body beforehand to prepare for my burial."*

The activist wing of the discipleship guild was irked by the gesture, and understandably so. Several of Jesus' followers scolded the woman for wasting the perfume when it could have been sold for a year's wages and given to the poor.[6] It's an airtight social-justice argument against excess. But Jesus shuts it down with a surprising statement in 14:6–7: "'Leave her alone,' said Jesus. 'Why are you bothering her? She has done a beautiful thing to me. The poor you will always have with you, and you can help them any time you want. But you will not always have me.'"

Even now, many sincere social-justice Christians simply can't abide Jesus' words regarding the poor here. Perhaps Mark (and Matthew and John) got the record wrong. I mean, did Jesus really condone this excessive expenditure on himself? Jesus just can't be flippantly endorsing the realities that create an economically oppressed class, right?

Right?

But our dilemma regarding Jesus' words might be resolved if we consider his vocation in light of his location.

On the latter point, his location, the story takes place against the backdrop of empire. Empire is where every teaching, every miracle, and every confrontation recorded in the Gospels happens. And this is in keeping with the entire biblical narrative; the

---

* Mark 14:8.

Bible is the story of people (Israel, Jesus, the church) in relation to a system (empire). In the Old Testament, we see sprawling empires like Egypt, Babylon, and Assyria. In the New Testament, Rome is the empire, and Jesus is smack-dab in the middle of its political drama.

Like I said, empire is the ocean humanity is swimming in, and Jesus' full humanity was immersed in that ocean.

In light of Jesus' location, I want to suggest a paraphrase of his statement about the poor: "For you always have *the empire* with you." As the epicenter of selfish power and control, empire is what insures that we will always have the poor with us. Empire always seeks wealth at the expense of the neediest; in so doing, it enacts policies of economic inequality. Individuals then absorb the values of empire, and personal entitlement, excess, and arrogance gradually and subtly trump the command to lift up the least of these.

And this rings true even today, doesn't it? While we must passionately seek to change the unjust systems we inhabit, it seems that short of divine intervention, empire is an inevitable reality. Some people somewhere will always seek systemic power in a sinful manner. And where the empire is, the poor are also sure to be.

Which brings us to Jesus' vocation. The woman with the alabaster jar was anointing Jesus for his burial. But Jesus approved this expenditure not as a policy favoring excess for special people but for this specific, historic moment. His burial would be the burial of the one true king. The luxurious ointment was fit for a king, but not any of the false kings of empire. Rather, it was intended for the divine king who rules over everything, including all those other kings, and whose true and lasting kingdom had just been inaugurated on earth as it is in heaven.

Divine intervention indeed.

"You will always have empire and its various oppressions with you." But Jesus in that moment ushered in a new reality with the divine potential to once and for all put an end to empire. The irony is rich. The disciples were royally ticked about wasting a decent donation for their little chapter of Occupy Rome, while the King in whose name all oppression shall cease was being anointed before their eyes.

It's as if Jesus was saying, "Yes, the empire is relentlessly ever-present, with its various oppressions. But there is still hope—true hope, lasting hope, ultimate hope. And I alone am it."

As we experience a great revealing of who we really are as American Christians, it is essential that we turn toward the even greater revealing of who Jesus really is. This is where our illusions might give way to the real, where the empire business in the world around us, in the church, and even in our hearts might be pushed back as the kingdom of God advances.

Because in the brilliance and beauty of Jesus the King lies the power for a new beginning—a flourishing faith and a prophetic hope for authentic and abiding change in the face of human empire, starting now and lasting into forever.

●　　　●　　　●

In an introduction to the book of Revelation, Pastor Brian Zahnd writes this:

> Jesus' lamb-like kingdom brings a saving alternative to the beast-like empires of the world. Revelation doesn't antici-pate the end of God's good creation—it anticipates the end of violent empire.[7]

The decline of Christian faith in the US presents us with an opportunity to embrace the realities that are being revealed. And what is being revealed, as with John's Apocalypse in the first century, is, I believe, how we have compromised with empire. These compromises are what we often prefer to remain blind to; they are what we tend to cover with our illusions. They are the ways, both large and small, that we get entangled with the empire pursuit of power and control, in which ego and ambition can evolve into deception and abuse, and even our pursuit of relevance can be a self-serving distraction from the kingdom work of humble, persevering, empowering service.

The power plays of empire business that make their way onto the American Christian scene and into our hearts can manifest in myriad ways. But one of the most overt is when the church seeks power in authoritarianism. Maybe you've come across this expression of empire leadership in your faith journey. I know I have.

Controlling Christianity

Brother Dawson knocked on our door repeatedly. It was the loudest knocking I'd ever heard. You could hear the rage in his tight fist.

He was yelling too, though I can't remember what he said. Most likely he was yelling for my father to answer the door, to come out and face him.

My father wasn't home. He was out doing the thing that had ignited Brother Dawson's rage—traveling up the East Coast with another leader from the church in Jasper, scouting locations where they and the group of disgruntled members they had assembled would go and start another church.

It was an act of treason, and Brother Dawson was on a mission to nip my father's betrayal in the bud. He got no answer as my mother, younger brother, and I hid in an upstairs bedroom, hands on our mouths to prevent any noise from giving us away.

Eventually he left.

Eventually we did too.

The problem is that even though we left this Texas cult, the brand of Christianity my father had learned there came with us. The teaching that formed the core of that church's doctrine and practice continued to form our lives too.

This teaching was the major theme of Brother Dawson's ministry. And the all-encompassing philosophy that he derived from it was the most potent draw on out-of-state folks like my parents to relocate to the little-known church in Jasper, Texas. It was a definitive doctrine, and Brother Dawson's writing and preaching on the topic might as well have been in the canon itself.

The primary prooftext for this teaching was Hebrews 4:12, which we always read in the King James Version: "For the word of God is quick, and powerful, and sharper than any two-edged sword, piercing even to the *dividing asunder* of soul and spirit, and of the joints and marrow, and is a discerner of the thoughts and intents of the heart."

While this phrase "dividing asunder" doesn't imply anything negative, the way Brother Dawson appropriated it for his ministry was critical and damaging.

For all of us in that Texas church, the teaching we simply referred to as "the dividing" outlined why we stood in such desperate need of the divinely appointed end-times apostles and prophets, particularly Brother Dawson and the elders: because they alone wielded the sword of the Word of God *as it is being revealed right now.* Anyone could pick up a Bible and try to understand it intellectually (intellect being a bad word to us spiritual people in Jasper), but if you wanted to get the Word of God for today, what God is saying right now at this crucial juncture in history, butted up, as it is, so close to history's end, then what you needed was to be divided asunder.

In the hands of God's apostles and prophets, the sword of the Word would divide you up and discern you at the deepest level of your spiritual being. With the threat of lukewarmness always lurking, and with the necessity for complete commitment and unconditional discipleship at an all-time high, the only way to endure till the end—and be saved—was to submit to the ongoing process of being divided asunder at the razor-sharp prophetic hands of Brother Dawson and the elders.

This discipleship vision demanded submission in every facet of one's life—spiritual, emotional, social, financial. It manifested in a practice that the elders called correction, chastisement, or "bishoping your soul"—a constant, hyperinvasive form of counseling that confronted members on every detail of their public and private lives, demanding conformity to the Jasper church's vision and values. Which were, like the vision and values of Brother Dawson himself, detailed, idiosyncratic, ever-evolving, and many, depending on what prophetic revelation happened to be in play at the moment.

The dividing was as pristine a theological mechanism for manipulation as one could dream up. It guaranteed absolute power to Brother Dawson and the elders. And it made this little-known church in Jasper, Texas, a bona fide cult.

•   •   •

The empire leadership I'm describing is one mark of cults, but it is not limited to groups that we might consider to be cults in the official sense.

Authoritarianism is a pervasive problem in American Christianity, existing in different ways and degrees across all denominations and movements. And I believe it is one of the easiest phenomena to connect to the church's decline, because part and parcel of our cultural moment is a shifting understanding of what constitutes good, true, and healthy authority. Those churches, movements, and streams that have fostered authoritarian leadership are most likely to push people away from Christian faith rather than draw them in or keep them close. You may have found yourself caught by this phenomenon, and it might be a significant reason for your own crisis of faith or exodus from the church. Maybe you've been burned by a bullying, perverted, or fraudulent leader you trusted and believed in. Maybe you've felt the clenched fist of leadership control over every detail of your life, and the shame and pain that go along with it.

Empire leadership has the opposite effect on people than it aims to have. In tightening its grip on those who believe, it drives them toward unbelief. And so much more so in this current moment, when cultural skepticism and antipathy toward the church and Christianity are increasing. When leadership breaks bad and seeks more power and control to stem the tide of decline, it is bound to result in more shipwrecked lives and ruined faith.

My life, and the lives of those I grew up with in a variety of church expressions, were devastated by the effects of empire business. Perhaps yours has been too.

If so, I am sorry. Deep emotional and spiritual damage are the legacy of authoritarianism in the church. It has left many of us picking up the pieces of our lives, trying to make sense of them, trying to keep hoping and believing, sometimes in vain.

The dividing was merely a mechanism for the empire business of arrogance and pride, which sacrifices lives on the altar of pathological ambition and self-aggrandizement. I witnessed this mechanism at work when Brother Dawson sought to bully my family into submission and prevent us from leaving. It was present every time he transgressed boundaries and invaded the lives of his followers, demanding conformity. It was present when he got close to leaders' wives that he was attracted to, telling them, "I can have any woman in this congregation I want." It was at work when he broke up marriages because they didn't reflect the values of the church—when one partner strayed from the elders' meticulous control over them.

But this mechanism was also at work when my father covertly grasped for control over a group of disgruntled members and plotted his treason. It was at work every time he shamed his future followers into submission and manipulated them into totally giving up their families, finances, and futures to follow the prophet of God. It was at work every time his reckless behavior wrecked his makeshift church startups, leaving ruined lives in his wake.

And on the American church scene, this authoritarian mechanism is also at work when a wildly successful megachurch prized for its relevance and innovation crumbles under a verbally and emotionally abusive leader. It is at work when pastors refuse to disclose their finances or reveal their salaries, even as they build fortunes on the backs of the struggling members of their churches. It is at work when preachers who claim to champion "biblical manhood" berate other men into submission and seek to blame, shame, and suppress women in the church. It is at work when leaders tell women who have suffered domestic abuse to let the men of the church handle it, and to learn to forgive and submit to their husbands anyway. It is at work when shepherding and discipleship become code words for the ego-stroking practice of bullying, the oldest power game in the book.

It is at work when repeated child sex abuse is uncovered in the history of a sprawling and influential church network, implicating leaders in the classic coverup tactic of counseling victims' families not to go to the police but to handle things in-house instead. It is at work when other famous leaders make light of this abuse and these victims and make much of protecting and perpetuating the ministry of the movement's leadership in the name of friendship. But this is not friendship. This is authoritarian protectionism, an abuse all its own. And it's not an anomaly. While child sex abuse and institutional coverup are now well documented in the Roman Catholic Church, some experts believe that the problem may be even worse, and more difficult to uncover, in the evangelical church.[8]

The empire business of lording it over others and acting as a master over them—something Jesus and the apostles consistently forbade in their New Testament call to servant leadership*—is all too common. And we are seeing much of this selfish power and control come to light in this moment of great revealing.

It is nothing less than an eruption of the real.

---

* Matthew 20:25ff.; 23:8ff.; 1 Peter 5:2ff.

Chapter 3

A Problem with Authority

All my life I've been looking for some spiritual place to call home. But I've always come up short. Because of that, I've also felt like an outsider—never wholly disconnected from the church's mainstream expressions, but never quite belonging to them either.

Perhaps that can be traced to my parents' decision to close their Miami church—where I had, for a significant period of my childhood, a sense of stability and belonging—and then move to a Texas cult. I'm not a professional therapist, but I suspect that decision is the fault line in the foundation of my life that later produced so much quaking instability and unease. It was the beginning of a pattern of always searching for "the city with foundations, whose architect and builder is God,"* but, like Father Abraham, forever walking in circles and never quite finding it.

Which is to say that I remember feeling at home in a place— Miami—and in a church—my parents' church plant. What I experienced was not just the innocence of youth or childish naivete but the deepest spiritual security and peace.

---

* Hebrews 11:10.

* * *

Everyone searches for a place of belonging and a spiritual home, whether or not we'd call it that. And that's what we often miss in the conversation about the decline of Christian faith in America, about the groups we like to call the nones and the dones. In this book so far we've talked a bit about the first group, but not as much about the second. If the nones are the unchurched, the dones are the dechurched. They are, in a unique sense, the spiritually homeless.

Josh Packard, a sociology professor, recently cowrote a book called *Church Refugees*, which addresses the dones as a subplot in the story of the decline of American Christianity. Like many of the nones, the dones live outside organized religion and often opt for a noninstitutional spiritual approach. But their defining trait is that they have left the church. After prolonged and committed involvement, often at various levels of leadership, they are finally and completely done. Without abandoning their Christian values, they have become the dechurched, the spiritually homeless. Of the sample group for his research, Packard writes:

> They thought the church was important enough to keep trying and trying. In fact, in our sample the average number of churches attended prior to leaving is more than four, spanning a number of years, indicating an astonishing commitment to the institution. The dechurched wanted to make the institution work, and they often worked for years for reform from within.[1]

And many of them are former leaders too—the ones who poured the most time and energy into the churches they served in various key roles. Packer adds, "if it were possible to stack up the energies and activities of the dechurched, that tower may well reach higher than the energy and activity that remain inside the walls of the institution."[2]

While the nones' emotional response to Christianity can run the gamut from confusion or disinterest to hostility or disgust, the dones' response is different: experiential, particular, heartfelt, grieving. The nones may never have experienced the beauty of what the church can be, but the dones typically have, which makes it all the more painful for them to leave. As a result, they are not flippant or ignorant and are very much sincere. The dones have simply arrived at a place where they can no longer remain part of the institutional church.

Maybe a better way of saying it is that though the dones leave church for a number of important reasons, perhaps all of them can be boiled down to institutionalism.

Institutionalism is really just another expression of empire business, because it pertains to how power and authority are used. Or better, while authoritarianism is about the impact of particular leaders on people, churches, and movements, institutionalism is about the culture of power and authority in a church or movement. This is not to say that institutions in and of themselves are bad. But when an institution's preservation becomes the be-all and end-all of its existence, it becomes corrupted.

When I interviewed Packard for this book and asked him to describe what the dones are really looking for, he said this: "We have church systems that privilege a very rigid type of authority. The dones are not asking for an absence of authority, they just want a different form. They want authority that comes from relationship and community accountability rather than authority that comes by virtue of a position or title. It's not erosion, it's just an evolution. And it's no different than what every other social institution is dealing with. The difference is simply that the church has been so much more slow to figure it out and adapt to it."[3]

Institutionalism—where the empire problem really lies—values the survival of the institution above all else. Problems with power and authority flow from there. Institutions must have rigid authority structures to maintain themselves, which necessarily means excluding groups that threaten it in some way. Institutionalism is obsessed with protecting the status quo, "the way we've always done things," to remain superficially healthy.

Packard's findings are clear that though the dones were once extraordinarily active and committed members and leaders of their churches,[4] they have quit the institution because of power and authority issues.

If you're on a similar path, then you know better than anyone that you did not take lightly the decision to quit. You've witnessed the empire business of institutionalism firsthand. And you just don't see the point of supporting it anymore.

One respondent to Packard's study of the dones said this: "The church over the last one hundred years has gone as institutions go. They become more cemented, and they gravitate toward maintenance, where they focus all of their energies on just keeping things going. Instead of existing for the world, they exist for themselves. And that, to me, didn't match the biblical narrative. It didn't match what I could see was needed and possible out in the world."[5]

As the decline of Christian faith in the US unfolds, there are many who refuse to embrace the opportunity it presents, closing their eyes to what is being revealed and instead seeking to stem the tide by reinforcing the status quo. When important things like a church organization or a ministry career are on the line, the impulse to give in to institutionalism can be incredibly hard to resist. Believe me, I know. It's far easier, and at least temporarily safer, to seek survival at all costs than to risk a revelation that might lead to repentance and radical change.

Always Reforming

After we escaped the clutches of Brother Dawson in Jasper, our family began a ministry odyssey that took us up the East Coast, first to Long Island, then northern New Jersey, and finally our northernmost resting place: cold and mountainous Vermont. But as our odyssey unfolded, the dividing mentality never left us, and the church communities that my father created along the way collapsed under his authoritarian leadership. And our family bore the burden, becoming increasingly isolated, broken, and unhealthy. I, perhaps, bore a particular burden as the main recipient of my father's most ferocious and relentless bishoping and dividing asunder, both because I was "called" to carry on the family legacy as the firstborn, and because I was increasingly prone to question all of it. Total conformity was the mandate, and my every difference in personality and perspective, no matter how minor, was treated as a dire threat. I was made to believe that something was deeply wrong with me, that I was, intrinsically, a problem. My father's "solution" was to systematically block me from social and educational opportunity, and to sabotage any potential success before it happened.

During this sojourn, my childish militancy increasingly gave way to adolescent turmoil and wrestling, especially because of the trauma and shame that I was internalizing.

In the midst of it all, I still loved Jesus deeply, spent hours in study and prayer, and continued to feel a strong sense of calling. Truly, it was my relationship with Christ that sustained me. And I was still searching diligently for a spiritual home, as lost as I felt at the time. Outwardly I did everything I could to uphold the family doctrine, and I had no intention of rebelling. But inwardly I was reckoning with all the damage and wondering where, if anywhere, I belonged.

As I entered my late teens, I discovered something that changed my life of faith especially and even changed our family dynamic.

I discovered the internet.

And then I discovered Reformed theology.

I belong to that in-between demographic that is not fully generation X and not quite millennial (generation Y maybe?), so I didn't grow up online. My access to information was limited, even more so because of my family's authoritarian tendencies. All I knew theologically was the form of charismatic Christianity I had grown up with, a movement marked by anti-intellectualism and the often bizarre and self-contradictory practice of prophetic revelation.

But then a cable was plugged into the back of the family computer. As I searched the web as part of my study, I landed on websites with lots of articles mentioning these dead guys Martin Luther, John Calvin, and Jonathan Edwards. (I had never read any Christian books by dead guys; how could they tell us what the Lord is saying *now*?) Shortly after that, I bought a copy of Luther's *The Bondage of the Will*. And soon I was won over to the powerful God and wrathful atonement of these sixteenth-century theological icons.

Reformed theology was the first version of Christianity I'd ever encountered that made both spiritual and intellectual sense. All through my adolescence, my faith was besieged by my brain as I analyzed all the things in our family doctrine that didn't add up or, worse, amounted to lies meant to cause havoc and harm in people's lives. I never would have admitted it then, but I was having a crisis of faith in which I sometimes wondered whether I could believe any of our family doctrine at all. In the darkest moments, I cried out to God to show me the truth, and stared out my bedroom window contemplating how I might run away from this lonely house in the middle of the cold Vermont countryside with no transportation and no friends.

So when I found the Reformed thinkers, I might as well have been grasping onto the bottom rung of a ladder to break a freefall. My love for Jesus and desire for a spiritual home were finally met with a sensible structure to support them. As strange as it might be for some of the people who know me now to hear, the powerful God of Calvin and Luther saved my faith. He may have even saved my life.

Reformed theology had something that all the flaky prophetic writing and rambling I'd grown up with lacked: substance. It gave me a sense of identity and independence for the first time, just as I was entering adulthood.

It gave me hope.

And it changed our family life too, as a thoughtful theological approach reduced some of the radical tendencies of the family faith. Even my father soon became as interested in this new direction as I was, and a degree of healing took place. We became closer, and I placed more of my trust in him.

●　　　●　　　●

Over the next half decade, my commitment to the Reformed vision of Christianity, and particularly the Calvinist vision of salvation, grew, and it was at least part of what led me to my wife, Kalen. The other part was snowboarding. At twenty-three, I was working full time as the snowboard director at a resort, and Kalen and I were the only two people our mutual friends knew who were both Christians and snowboarders. (Vermont was the least religious state in the nation, after all.) Naturally they assumed we were meant for each other. On the first chairlift ride on our first platonic nondate, I, ever so smoothly, asked Kalen if she'd ever heard of Reformed theology. She had, grew up with the stuff in fact, and the rest is blissful history.

Once married, Kalen and I started attending a midsize Baptist church near where we lived. But this Baptist church was nothing like other Baptist churches, at least none that I'd ever heard of. It was theologically astute and unapologetically Calvinist. It was a harbinger of the now-popular Gospel-Centered movement. And it was all of these things in the most conservative sense imaginable.

Best of all, for me at least, there was no charismatic flakiness, no weak seeker-friendliness, no contrived relevance. The senior pastor who had planted the church a decade earlier famously committed to build it only on the gospel—no gimmicks. There wasn't a rock band, laser show, or youth group called Shockwave, not to mention any bizarre spiritual manifestations in the middle of a service. I felt I could finally and completely leave the East Texas church and its bishoping behind.

What's more, the people seemed supercommitted—they were serious about their faith and their church and had a genuine sense of community. Kalen and I made good friends there. I had a wonderful mentor. I learned a lot about ministry. And my parents even joined us, attending for a time.

After attending for a bit, Kalen and I approached one of the pastors about baptism and membership. Since it was a Baptist church, we knew that Kalen's Congregationalist infant baptism wasn't going to cut it if we wanted to become members. And besides, we had been going through a lot of changes in our first year of marriage, and that included some significant spiritual change in Kalen's heart and life—significant enough, we thought, to mark with a bona fide "believer's baptism."

But then something strange happened in our first prebaptism meeting. The senior pastor suggested that Kalen had not been truly saved, truly regenerate, before these latest changes had occurred. He even suggested that I had engaged in "missionary dating"—courting and marrying Kalen while she was yet unconverted. Which, honestly, was pretty devastating to think about, since what had drawn me to my wife in the first place was her humble, sincere faith and the spiritual ground we shared, the very things that caused our mutual friends to introduce us. (It was also just inaccurate, since I was going through a lot of the same changes she was, my childhood believer's-baptism card notwithstanding.)

So we winced at this but laughed it off. We were new. And then it was full steam ahead to the day of the big baptism. Kalen had prepared a beautiful testimony of childhood faith that had been tested by a difficult home and family life, coming to greater maturity in our first year of being married. While she waited her turn to speak and get dunked in the baptistery, the young man sitting next to her whispered a question.

"How many times is this for you?"

"Getting baptized, you mean?" Kalen replied.

"Yeah."

"Oh. My first time—you know, as an adult. How about you?"

"It's my third time, all of them here at this church. But this time I think I'm truly saved."

That's when we started to get nervous.

The Status Quo Illusion

One thing this apocalypse is revealing is the fear-based institutional control many churches use to keep people inside their doors. But it is also revealing that this control will never really be enough to stop the trend of decline in church attendance and religious practice. And even if such control seems to work for a time, it will ultimately fail because preserving the status quo forfeits the opportunity to make necessary reforms. Spiritually speaking, institutionalism hardens our hearts to the invitation God is extending to embrace a flourishing faith.

Perhaps this hardness of heart is best seen in a popular way of interpreting the data of religious decline. This perspective holds that the majority of those who claim some sort of Christian spirituality or belief but do not attend church, or have left the church, are merely nominal Christians.

Christians in name only.

Not real Christians, because real Christians faithfully attend an organized church no matter what.

Pretty harsh, right? Especially if you, like me, have often felt like an outsider in mainstream churches. Especially if you, like me, have longed for a spiritual home but have struggled to find a place to belong.

The argument goes like this: as the culture continues to become post-Christian or post-Christendom, and religious pluralism and secularism gain ground, people who have claimed Christianity only because of social convenience or as a matter of family identity will be weeded out. And good riddance! These, they say, are "mushy Christians" who are "just indifferent."[6] The American church is clarifying, or perhaps purifying, itself, and we needn't worry. Keep calm and carry on with business as usual.

This argument could, and often does, employ one of the popular ways of preaching a Calvinist view of salvation: only the "truly converted, truly regenerate, truly elect" will remain affiliated with the church amid the decline. Biblically, 1 John 2:19 becomes a useful prooftext (taken out of context, of course) to support this statistics-conscious sermon: "They went out from us, but they did not really belong to us. For if they had belonged to us, they would have remained with us; but their going showed that none of them belonged to us." One popular author recently tweeted that the main reason millennials are leaving the church is simply because they are unregenerate.

I call this perspective the "status quo illusion," because it is an effective way to preserve the status quo by dismissing the realities of the decline. Without any data to back it up, it invents a single motivation for all those who have left the church or the faith, rendering them a "mushy" unwanted class that we're better off without. It pays no mind to the data about the dones, not to mention their personal stories. It turns its head and walks on by as if they don't exist, happy to exclude them.

The status quo illusion avoids panic over declining numbers and pushes back on the suggestion that Christian faith in America is dying or collapsing. And that's good! But it also arrogantly dismisses reality and so avoids the great revealing that is upon us. It is a power move, one that sidesteps reflection that risks change. And it is an illusion because the success or stability that it boasts about is achieved by operating contrary to the kingdom way, the Jesus way. It says, "We don't need them anyway. Let them walk," when Jesus says, "Come to me, all you who are weary and burdened, and I will give you rest."* It initiates a containment strategy when Jesus goes outside the gate to pursue at any cost the one lost sheep, leaving the corralled in-group behind.†

When Jesus needed to explain what the kingdom of God is like to the religious institution of his day, he usually launched into stories about inclusion in which the religious class is passed over in favor of outsiders, the unclean, even unbelievers. Stories like this one in Luke 14:

> A certain man was preparing a great banquet and invited many guests. At the time of the banquet he sent his servant to tell those who had been invited, "Come, for everything is now ready." But they all alike began to make excuses . . .
>
> The servant came back and reported this to his master. Then the owner of the house became angry and ordered his servant, "Go out quickly into the streets and alleys of the town and bring in the poor, the crippled, the blind and the lame."
>
> "Sir," the servant said, "what you ordered has been done, but there is still room."
>
> Then the master told his servant, "Go out to the roads and country lanes and compel them to come in, so that

---

* Matthew 11:28–30.
† Luke 15:1–7.

my house will be full. I tell you, not one of those who were invited will get a taste of my banquet."*

While it would be easy to dismiss such a parable as a response to Jewish unbelief in the first century, that would be missing the point entirely. Jesus was not so much about the business of establishing a new religion as reforming the current religion, not inventing Christianity but fulfilling the faith of Israel. His pointed confrontation—"not one of those who were invited will get a taste of my banquet"—is not merely a vindictive response to rejection. It is a protest against the exclusionary practices of the first-century Israelite religion. The religious impulse that rejected Jesus was the same impulse that quarantined "the poor, the crippled, the blind and the lame" to "the roads and country lanes." And the same table practices that excluded gentiles, women, tax collectors, and sinners also later excluded the Messiah himself from Israel's table (and had him executed on the empire's cross), which is why Jesus shockingly fellowshiped at the table with all of those unwelcome groups.

The first-century Israelite religion was a mess of institutionalism. Its status and stability were threatened by this inclusive Messiah, its power compromised by his disruptive presence. Jesus rocked the status quo by embracing the nones and dones of his day. And not just embracing them but saying that the kingdom of God will be more like fraternizing with *them* than feasting with *us*.

The Messiah and his good news disrupted the empire business of the Israelite religion at every turn.

---

* Verses 16–24.

* * *

As the years went by serving at that Calvinist Baptist church, we got a clearer picture of the institutional structure at work. The multiple baptisms—all taking place *there*, not because of denominational transfer, as in Kalen's case—were normative, rooted in a theology of predestinarian "true conversion." There was an ingrained anxiety among the members and attenders, who were never sure whether their lives manifested the right kind or amount of behavioral fruit to prove that God had irresistibly saved and regenerated their souls. An unrelenting emphasis on our total moral depravity and hell-deserving condition was preached from the pulpit, with the intention of producing a kind of Puritan "anxious bench" in the pews as people grappled with their heinous sin. The high school kids we worked with as youth group leaders sat confused and discouraged about the possibility of their own salvation. Most of them didn't feel they could even call themselves Christians. Small children's innocent professions of faith were disregarded by the adults; they were unregenerate until proven otherwise, and we would have to wait and see.

The church's theology of gender roles in the home and in the church, taken to extremes, created a culture where gifted women were sternly and systematically excluded from ministry and family decision-making. Many women in the church carried a heaviness about them. One of them was my wife. The oppressiveness of this culture finally moved her to insist that we leave, despite the friends we had and the investment we'd made. The hurt and consternation that I saw her experience moved me to follow her lead.

All of these experiences indicated how authority functioned in the culture of the church to create a rigid in-group to insure the institution's survival. The heavyhanded exclusion of women kept the right men with the right theology in control. The relentless preaching on depravity and hell kept members and attenders corralled. And anxiety about genuine conversion and regeneration (and the practice of multiple baptisms) kept people coming back to the pastors for more, because they alone held the keys to the kingdom. The pastors taught that one of the primary fruits of genuine conversion was "love of the brethren," which, they said, is seen most clearly in diligent financial support of the church. What better way to insure that the church is always sustainable—even wealthy—than by linking the tithe to one's eternal destiny?

As much as I'd thought that I'd found a home in the theology of Luther, Calvin, and Edwards, I'd come up short again.

Apparently I have a problem with authority. Not in a rebellious punk-rock sense (though I wish that were true, because it would make me a lot cooler than I am) but in the sense that my experiences with authoritarianism have also made me deeply resistant to the exclusionary tendencies of institutionalism.

And I'm not alone. The cultural shift we are witnessing revolves, at least in part, around similar problems with authority. And perpetuating institutionalism is not going to prevent this eruption of the real from taking place.

Kalen and I decided that the in-group obsession was excluding too many of the people we loved, both inside and outside that church, from meeting Jesus. The ideology was suffocating people. We desperately desired something different, a gospel and a community committed to including nones, dones, and whomever else the Lord might call.*

---

* Acts 2:39.

We didn't care if leaving made us unconverted, unregenerate, nonelect, or nominal in the eyes of the in-group.

When I interviewed Josh Packard for this book and asked what he thought of the status quo illusion and exclusionary responses to the dones, here's what he said:

> I find the idea of "nominal" Christianity to be vile and offensive at every level. To talk about the idea of nominal Christianity is to fundamentally destroy relationships with people who are on your side! Additionally, it's just wrong. I've implored people with this perspective on numerous occasions to show me the data supporting their position. They don't, because they can't. That data doesn't exist. This is a made up, ideological position, not one rooted in reality.
>
> Finally, and most important, this perspective discounts the wisdom of God and the movement of the Holy Spirit. If we really think that God is in charge and that the Holy Spirit moves in important and powerful ways, we need to be attuned to the things that are going on that we don't have control over. People are not static. They change with the various seasons of their lives. Dropping this label of "nominal" on them paints a picture of someone who *is*, not someone who is becoming. When I sign my books, I inscribe them with "Remember, God makes ALL things new." That includes me and you and everyone else too.[7]

The status quo illusion is indeed an ideological position, one that simply will not last as this great revealing of kingdom reality continues to unfold.

Chapter 4

American Empire

In the early days of my Reformed and Calvinist fervor, I made a mistake that has stuck with me. I'm sure I made a bunch of them back then, but this one, in my mind, represents the big problem with my deeply held beliefs at that time. This big problem eventually was revealed to me and caused my wife and me to move on from that exclusionary Baptist church and its harmful institutionalism. But years earlier, before I met Kalen, I wasn't aware of any problem. I was just thrilled to have grabbed hold of something solid in my spiritual searching.

It was a couple of years after the September 11th attacks, just before President Bush and Congress issued a declaration of war against Iraq. I joined a friendly political discussion in the staff room of the ski resort where I was working. I knew that most of my friends and coworkers were politically progressive, if not ideologically, then just by osmosis, being decent people who cared about the planet and the poor and wore Patagonia. This was Vermont, after all, a haven for peace-loving liberal folks and their causes. (That the Green Mountain State gave us Ben and Jerry's Ice Cream and Senator Bernie Sanders is no accident.)

Deep down, I admired my friends and their progressiveness,

which they seemed to inhabit so effortlessly. But I was also filled with ideas about God and politics culled from the theologies of Luther and Calvin (and their modern representatives) and the rantings of conservative talk radio. It was quite a cocktail, and it placed me in an antagonistic position—one that I was simultaneously insecure and prideful about. I'd like to think I wasn't a jerk, but I was at least overconfident in order to mask that insecurity. I used harsh words and a sharp tone. I was defensive. Looking back on this episode, I can almost feel my zeal edging into jerkiness, and it makes me wince.

After trying to shut down the argument being made by my good friend, I set my sights on the new ski instructor we had just hired, a women's studies graduate student who was about to go out to teach a telemark lesson. She sat quietly as I peppered her with questions: "Don't you know Saddam Hussein harbors Al Qaeda? Have you read Bin Laden's manifesto? Regardless of whether there's WMD, do you really think we can win the war on terror if we don't change the regime in Iraq and gain ground for democracy in the Middle East?"

If it weren't for the snowboard pants I was wearing, you'd think I was an FBI interrogator.

She was steady in the face of my questioning. It had to be intimidating to have one of your bosses getting all political on your first day of work, right before your first lesson. Nevertheless, calmly and simply she answered, "I'm a pacifist. I know it's not practical, but I just think war is wrong in all circumstances."

My confidence melted, and I was dumbfounded. I could have argued against her position, but I couldn't argue with her heart. Something about the peace she was talking about felt true. What was I supposed to do with *that*?

This exchange didn't change my views or curb my talk radio habit. But my verbal onslaught indicated a crack in the bedrock of my new beliefs, because the God I had come to believe in approved of the American empire's violent reactions to the world's brokenness. He was a God who wanted war. I wanted war too.

And I was wrong.

Lukewarm in Laodicea

Central to the East Texas church's culture was the concept of the lukewarm Christian. The concept was drawn, of course, from Revelation 3, which gives us the last in a series of seven messages to seven influential churches in Asia Minor. Jesus, speaking through the apostle John, saved his strongest words for last: "I know your deeds, that you are neither cold nor hot. I wish you were either one or the other! So, because you are lukewarm— neither hot nor cold—I am about to spit you out of my mouth. You say, 'I am rich; I have acquired wealth and do not need a thing.' But you do not realize that you are wretched, pitiful, poor, blind and naked. I counsel you to buy from me gold refined in the fire, so you can become rich; and white clothes to wear, so you can cover your shameful nakedness; and salve to put on your eyes, so you can see."*

Like many things that become Christian cliches, the metaphor of lukewarmness is usually taken out of context. It becomes a general warning against not having a hot enough faith, a committed enough walk with the Lord, a holy enough lifestyle,

---

* Revelation 3:15–18.

and instead being only halfheartedly devoted. Jesus hates this halfheartedness, preachers say, so you should rededicate your life to him or come to the front of the church and get delivered from whatever sin or spiritual laziness afflicts you. Jesus would rather you be cold or hot—either a licentious heathen or a totally on-fire follower. No more messing around in the middle.

(I sometimes wonder how many sincere but struggling Christians actually have chosen the cold option as a result of this browbeating.)

The East Texas church added to this cliche a more extreme benchmark for what it means to be committed and on-fire: submit to the discipleship process led by the last days apostles and prophets, or else face eternal death and hell when the end comes. It was an ultimate us-versus-them proposition, consigning all Christians not part of the move of God in Jasper, Texas, to lukewarmness and likely destruction.

But the context of this warning to the church in Laodicea leads to a much different emphasis than individual commitment and spiritual holiness.

Our first clue comes in the fact that the message is addressed to a church—a body of Christians. Something was wrong collectively.

Our second clue is what Jesus quotes this group as saying: "You say, 'I am rich; I have acquired wealth and do not need a thing.'" The something wrong in this church was wrapped up in its economic status: it was wealthy and self-reliant.

And our third clue has to do with the metaphor itself. Why was Jesus, through John, using the metaphor of lukewarmness in the first place? As with most things in Scripture, we have to look at the historical context—the geography and background of the city. To the north of Laodicea, Hierapolis had healthy hot springs, and to the south, Colossae had cold springs that were clean and refreshing to drink from. But Laodicea had perpetual problems with its water supply, which was brought by aqueduct six miles from the south. By the time the water reached Laodicea, it had become lukewarm. It was tepid, unclean, and undrinkable, the kind of water that makes you sick, that you might spit or vomit out of your mouth, as Jesus is said to do, metaphorically speaking, with the entire Laodicean church.[1]

Jesus' words here, rather than a call to hot personal commitment and revival, confront a social sickness in the church that springs from embracing the lifestyle of the wealthy and elite. This sickness is especially hard to detect because the church appears to be numerically healthy and self-sufficient. But with respect to the gospel and the kingdom mission, it is "wretched, pitiful, poor, blind and naked."[*]

To be spiritually healthy is to be either cold or hot. To be spiritually sick is to be lukewarm. In the words of New Testament scholar Michael Gorman, "Lukewarmness is not an ancient metaphor for indifference. The text, therefore, does not present a spectrum with two extremes—hot (for Jesus) and cold (against Jesus)—and a wishy-washy middle. Rather, it presents two antithetical points, the first of which is illustrated with two images, hot water and cold water. Both of these are pleasing and beneficial, while lukewarm water is precisely the opposite, disgusting to taste and not salutary. 'Lukewarm' here means so prosperous and supposedly self-sufficient (3:17) as to be completely out of fellowship with Jesus."[2]

---

[*] Revelation 3:17.

The lukewarm Laodicean church was compromised by the status quo ways of the Roman Empire. They were, according to Gorman, "not only participating with the status quo when necessary as a means of survival, but fully embracing the lifestyle and values of the elite and powerful."[3] And in this sense, lukewarmness is a temptation that the church has always faced, right up to the present day. The living water that Jesus offers can quickly become tainted by indulging in the wealth and power of the empire.

And that's because empire wealth and power are signs of allegiance to a kingdom other than the kingdom of God. The Laodiceans' spiritual malady was not a lack of individual moral or spiritual commitment but the collective compromise with empire values that put them out of step with the kingdom of God.

They had bought into empire business.

•   •   •

When we look at this warning to the Laodiceans in light of the theme of Revelation, an interesting picture emerges. Revelation is not, as we've noted, a timeline for the last days but rather a poetic protest against the Roman Empire in light of the church's endings and beginnings. That includes, of course, the final victorious ending and beginning—a resurrection of the dead, a final judgment, and a new heaven and a new earth. But Revelation is fundamentally, as one historian noted, a "politically charged book."[4] Some scholars have zeroed in on the real identity of "the Beast" in Revelation—not the smooth end-times politician depicted in the Left Behind series but the emperor of Rome in the late first century. And the mark of the Beast, 666? Quite possibly a discreet and clever code: the numerical value of the Greek and Latin letters in Nero Caesar's name.[5] Yes, that Nero, the extravagantly wealthy and horrifically violent emperor of Rome who persecuted and murdered Christians by the thousands and began a vicious war against the Jews that resulted in the destruction of the temple and the razing of Jerusalem in AD 70.

But just as Revelation was relevant to the empire in the apostle John's day, it is relevant to the empire in our day: the American empire.

Which means it's relevant to *us*.

Seeing the church as situated in a political empire that calls for kingdom protest may be a new, or at least different, idea for some of us. We might prefer to think of the church as apolitical or perhaps as comfortably aligned with one side of the political conversation. But I wonder how our perspective might change if we put on these apocalyptic optics. No sin, no mistake, is more serious in John's Apocalypse than the sin of compromising with the oppressive wealth and violent warfare of the empire. This is the essence of what it means to be lukewarm—and vom-worthy to Jesus the King. And this diagnosis is consistent with the warp and woof of the prophetic tradition from Old Testament to New.

For this reason, Old Testament scholar Walter Brueggemann has repeatedly described the American empire with two simple words: military consumerism. I'd say that sums up the Laodicean church and the apocalyptic protest of Revelation quite well.

Is the Christian faith in America compromised with the empire values of military consumerism? Is my faith compromised? Is yours?

I believe our apocalyptic moment is a pointer to this compromise, an opportunity to see it clearly so we can make a radical kingdom change.

What Would Jesus Carry?

My cringeworthy debate in the ski resort staff room manifested a popular perspective that merged evangelical theology with political warmongering, Christian values with a right-wing agenda. I had bought into a perspective that made me, the lone Christian in that awkward debate, less Christian than the non-Christian ski instructor who gently held her impractical pacifist ground. She argued for peace in a peaceful way; I argued for war in a combative way. I'm not saying that the only Christian view is absolute political pacifism. But I am saying that one of us in that debate was much closer to defending the good news (gospel) of peace, and it wasn't me.

But even then I was in the early stages of a process that led, several years later, to a break with that theological and political merger when my wife and I left the Calvinist Baptist church. We departed from a God who aligns with violent empire, who wants war, and we started a journey toward something different.

An episode served as the last straw for us. At the home group where I was an assistant leader to the senior pastor, it was my turn to facilitate. Right after the snack 'n' chat time (because *every* home group has a snack 'n' chat), the senior pastor asked me to pray. But he didn't just ask me to pray to start the study time like usual. He asked me to pray about a famous Christian leader who had passed away that day, a leader who was one of the early founders of the Religious Right, a Republican culture warrior whose public campaigning against immorality (and relentless opposition to liberal politicians) had earned him wealth and political power. This man represented all the things I was growing uncomfortable with in the merger of Christian faith with a right-wing political agenda.

The senior pastor began with an impromptu eulogy: "I received news that a great man of God died today. He was a warrior for righteousness in America, especially in the battle against immorality of every kind. He was a faithful witness to the truth, and he reminded us of what America once was and what it could be again someday."

Then the pastor requested that I lead the group in thanking God for this faithful warrior and his great work, and to pray for peace for his family.

Preceding his request were hours of private conversations I'd been having with him about my growing concerns with the church and the transition happening in my faith, including the political dimension. So, yes, *of course* I felt sorrow for this famous leader's family in their loss. But a knot grew in my stomach at the thought of publicly honoring him for a persona and an agenda that I strongly disagreed with. It felt deeply dishonest. And as I regretfully mustered up a simple prayer, I knew that I had been manipulated into going against my conscience. He'd put me on the spot to teach me a lesson.

The culture of this church enthusiastically endorsed the lukewarm compromise of American Christianity, particularly the kind of power held by the famous leader in question. On top of that, it presented a dilemma that proved impossible to overcome—the dilemma of harshly excluding the culture and friends we had come to embrace. My war-loving tirade to that peace-loving ski instructor was the bad fruit of this church's theological root, and it would not serve us in the future. For the sake of the people outside the church that we loved, and for the sake of a mission that might welcome and include them, we needed to leave.

The 2016 political season saw one of the most shocking and offensive presidential candidates in history experience a meteoric rise to popularity. The attraction seemed to be his brazen, no-nonsense, hardline stance on a number of conservative political issues, including abortion, gun rights, immigration, the military, and international trade. He also happens to be a millionaire real-estate tycoon, a man who has lived his life indulging in the oppressive wealth of the empire. And despite his relentless sexist, racist, and xenophobic rhetoric and policymaking, he claimed faith in Christ throughout his campaign and boasted of his belovedness among "the evangelicals."

We are living in Laodicea.

In a strange turn of events, the son of the famous Religious Right leader that I said a halfhearted prayer for in that home group was one of the first well-known Christians to give his wholehearted endorsement to this Republican candidate. I suppose it shouldn't have been surprising. Because this same man, the chancellor of the conservative Christian college founded by his culture-warrior father, is famous for telling his students to take up arms against potential domestic terrorists: "It just blows my mind that the president of the United States [says] that the answer to circumstances like that is more gun control . . . I've always thought that if more good people had concealed-carry permits, then we could end those Muslims before they walked in, and killed them. I just wanted to take this opportunity to encourage all of you to get your permit. We offer a free course. Let's teach them a lesson if they ever show up here."[6]

In that same address, he even joked that he had a gun in his back pocket and didn't know whether it was okay for him to take it out. All to thunderous applause.

Has American Christianity become compromised with the military consumerism of the empire? Has my faith become compromised? Has yours?

These military consumerist expressions of faith serve as an eruption of the real, revealing to us, in the starkest terms, the unholy merger between Christian faith and an American politic drunk on power, wealth, and war.

●   ●   ●

In *Reversed Thunder*, his book on Revelation, Pastor Eugene Peterson says, "The perennial ruse is to glorify war so that we accept it as a proper means of achieving goals. But it is evil. It is opposed by Christ. Christ does not sit on the red horse, ever."[7] Brian Zahnd adds these comments to Peterson's: "Christians are called to believe that cosuffering love and the divine word are all Christ needs to overcome evil. A fallen world addicted to war does not believe this, but the followers of Jesus do . . . or should! If Jesus conquers evil by killing his enemies, he's just another Caesar. But the whole point of John's Revelation is that Jesus is nothing like Caesar! The war of the Lamb looks nothing like the war of the Beast. Jesus is not like Caesar; Jesus does not wage war like Caesar. To miss this point is to misunderstand everything the Apocalypse is trying to reveal!"[8]

Emperor Nero is the one who wages bloody war on his enemies, subduing them in vicious and grotesque ways, be they zealous Jews in Jerusalem or subversive Christians living in the shadow of the empire. Jesus, by the way, had already prophesied to his Israelite brothers and sisters that they should not fight the empire with the tools of empire: "As he approached Jerusalem and saw the city, he wept over it and said, 'If you, even you, had only known on this day *what would bring you peace*—but now it is hidden from your eyes. The days will come upon you when your enemies will build an embankment against you and encircle you and hem you in on every side. They will dash you to the ground, you and the children within your walls. They will not leave one stone on another, because you did not recognize the time of God's coming to you.'"*

I believe we find ourselves in the midst of a great revealing of who we really are as American Christians, and who Jesus and his kingdom really are in the midst of it all. Perhaps we even find ourselves at a crossroads, a moment of opportunity when we might be able to recognize and embrace "what would bring you peace" amid the wars being waged by the empire, and the wars about to be waged. Yes, this moment of apocalyptic revealing entails a necessary ending to the status quo, the institutionalized and exclusionary "way we've always done things." But it just might be leading us to a brilliant new beginning and a flourishing faith.

Has American Christian faith been compromised? Has my faith? Has yours?

I would venture to say yes.

But there's another way, if we have eyes to see and ears to hear before it's too late.

---

* Luke 19:41–44, emphasis mine.

Chapter 5

This Is How My World Ends

I am twenty years old, and we are on a family trip to Arizona to visit friends and followers of my father. I am not in college, because college is forbidden in our family doctrine, and my father has suppressed my lifelong desire to study writing or theology or to go to art school. I have no educational or vocational opportunities. I won't even take Bible school classes until after I'm married.

I am discovering Reformed theology, teaching myself and thinking for myself, and beginning to leave the family doctrine behind. But I am not rebelling. I know that if I do, my relationship with my family will suffer and my relationship with my father will end. It's simply unthinkable. I see it as my role to submit to this suppressing of my gifts and sabotaging of my potential in order to maintain the peace and togetherness of the family. I am loyal, compliant, even at twenty. I have been effectively bishoped.

One morning on this trip, my father calls an impromptu Bible study in our hotel room, a common practice with our family and with whoever happened to be following my father at the time, such as these folks we were visiting in Arizona. This Bible study is called not so much for our sakes as for theirs. My father has a message for them, and this cross-country trip presents a golden opportunity to deliver it in the most direct way possible. So they arrive, and in typical fashion he distributes handouts, which are almost too thick for the staples. Which means this Bible study will be long. (I always count the pages when he's not looking in my direction.)

The title of this handout is "The False God of Education," and after only a few minutes it dawns on me why this meeting has been called: our friends have been planning to send their kids to a charter school in the hope that they can get into a good college. This Bible study is an attack to preempt these plans. With a good deal of convenient prooftexting (and no shortage of bold-print vitriol), my father's paper makes the case that all organized forms of education—Christian or not—constitute idolatry and are unspiritual. More to the point, they are dangerously independent of his authority, and his authority is what he hopes to impose on these friends, who had been longtime and recently lapsed followers of his ministry.

The meeting is long, and our friends are visibly upset. The situation is painfully awkward. And I can tell that my father perceives from my pained silence that I don't agree with him.

In our parked car after the Bible study, he instructs everyone to leave but me. I know what is coming. In keeping with his pattern, he loudly confronts my quiet disagreement. I reassure him that I only think people should be able to discern their own views on these things and I don't wish to oppose him in any way. But he persists and his anger turns to wide-eyed rage and he is asking me what my problem is and when am I ever going to change and how dare I go against the word God has given him. He shames me for my unspirituality, calls my faith and commitment into question, keeps coming at me with accusation, and something is rising up in me and I don't know what it is. Until it erupts. "I can't do this anymore!" And I open the door and I am weeping and running and I don't know where to.

I stop, eventually, and he drives the car to where I am, and I get back in—not just into the vehicle but into the pattern that has been happening for years and will continue until my emotional and spiritual death become not just shadows but devastating and final realities.

I get back into thinking that everything—myself, my future— revolves around my ministry call, just like my father's life did. If I want his acceptance and approval, I need to pursue that call with abandon, like a good disciple. Though I have the opportunity to opt out by staying out of that car, it is an end I can't face, a death I can't endure—yet.

When it comes to this calling on my life, the stakes are so high.

●　　　●　　　●

After we left the Calvinist Baptist church, I found myself, yet again, wandering, searching for a spiritual home, a place to belong. I had invested so much into this church, and I'd seen my calling begin to find fulfillment. There were opportunities available to me there, opportunities to move from small group and youth group ministry into pastoral ministry, but we had to walk away from all of it. I was twenty-eight years old, and I could feel my calling slipping away. I needed to find a decent career, we wanted to start a family, and it seemed like ministry just wouldn't fit into that future. And I was just tired. We had served and led for nearly four years, from the time we got married, and we were exhausted. It was hard to muster up any desire, not to mention any energy, to make another investment that would take years to mature.

I remember being unable to sleep one night and finding myself in my little townhouse office room, praying. My prayer moved me to the floor, becoming something more like begging. I was begging God to allow this calling to find fulfillment again, to manifest in ministry again. I was crying and telling him that I was willing, that I was available. But then I issued an ultimatum. Yes, I issued an ultimatum to God: "Lord, I love you. I want to serve you with my life. I know I'm called to do that. But I have only one more attempt left in me. After everything in my childhood, after all we invested in this church only to come up short again, the next attempt will be my last. So, please, God: make it last!"

Best Intentions

My search for a spiritual home continued. Though we were tired, something kept us seeking a place in the church, and a way to serve God's people and the world. We didn't have any intention to start something on our own, at least not at first, but as we kept praying and seeking, things just began to happen. Some friends who were also in transition joined us for an informal home group at our townhouse, then more friends joined in and we began to feel that maybe this was exactly what we were looking for.

Over the next year and a half, we became more and more intentional about our worship and study times together, eventually acknowledging that this was becoming church for us. We were all casually attending other churches on Sundays, but we agreed to start doing our home meetings on Sundays instead and make that our primary church commitment. And then things started to get really exciting.

This was at a pivotal moment in the American church. Not only was the reality of religious decline setting in, but so was a corresponding openness to new forms and expressions and ways of "doing church." From theology to worship format to missional engagement, it seemed everything was changing, and our burgeoning church group found itself right in the middle of it. I began to feel like this was it, this was the home I'd always been looking for. This was the movement I wanted to be a part of forever.

And when the time came to go public as a church plant, I embraced the transition from home group leader to lead pastor with abandon, feeling the rush and relief of my calling finally coming to fruition. Kalen's struggles with the church were resolving too, and she led and served alongside me in such a beautiful way. We formed a leadership team to help steer and serve the community as it grew. There was such joy and togetherness, especially at the beginning.

Coinciding with this excitement was something less positive. The year 2008 was not a good time for the US economy. And almost immediately after we decided to plant the church, both Kalen and I faced unexpected career changes in the form of a layoff for her and the loss of salaried status for me. This was not ideal for two people about to plant a church. But we decided to sell our townhouse and move into the most economically challenged neighborhood in Burlington (Vermont's largest city and the least religious place in the US at the time). Because the housing market had plummeted, we took a sizable loss on the sale of our home. All in all, it was a huge financial risk.

We mortgaged our lives to plant this church. But we were convinced that God was with us, and we believed he would provide whatever we needed to see it through. I felt a profound sense of gratitude that God had accepted my prayer for one last shot. I knew—I was certain—that this was it.

As we went public, my family decided to become part of our church. My parents wanted to be as involved as possible. I was hesitant about their involvement, especially about my father's influence. But he seemed supportive, and things seemed to be getting better in our relationship again. With the best of intentions, I trusted him, included him, and hoped against hope that we had finally put the old dividing season to rest.

Over the next few years, things weren't perfect—in my father's behavior and in the church itself. But the negative stuff was manageable, and there was so much good. And the church grew. We were amazed by how it grew! We joined an evangelical denomination and became something of a model for a missional church in such a progressive city in post-Christian New England. We were engaging culture with our unique service format and creative outreach, we were including people who were unchurched and dechurched, and we were making an impact on the city, to the degree that the alternative weekly (known to occasionally slam local evangelicals) praised our efforts. We had a cutting edge website, along with amazing graphic design and a strong social media game. But most important, we saw the Lord do some amazing things as we loved and served the people he brought to us. New Christians were baptized; those who had struggled were recommitting their lives to Jesus; young couples were counseled and married; babies were born, including our first two girls; conflicts and disagreements were reconciled.

But the final year of our church plant brought a drastic shift in this momentum. The city of Burlington had become something of a church-planting hotbed, creating struggles for sustainability among a small pool of potential congregants. And conflicts in our own congregation that were manageable before seemed to grow more personal and damaging. People started leaving, opting for the missional church down the street. And the public perception of our church grew more and more sour.

As our numbers declined, so did the church budget. Over the year, we were forced to downsize our worship space from a cool warehouse to a community center to a midday slot at a Methodist church until we were finally meeting in a living room again. And the already tenuous financial situation that my wife and I were facing worsened as our partial stipend, which sustained us along with part-time nonprofit jobs, was in serious jeopardy. By the end, it was unsustainable. And right smack dab in the middle of that final year, our second child was born.

But these external factors, as stressful as they were, paled in comparison with the struggle taking place within me. Wounds were reopened, and the fear of losing the belonging and the calling I had finally found nearly consumed me. I had tried so hard not to repeat my parents' mistakes. I had spent every waking moment and every sleepless night building a church that could become stable and sustainable, with good accountability and a solid reputation and a well-organized structure. This was no fly-by-night, thrown-together thing; it was my life's work. My last attempt! But it was falling apart all around me, and I just couldn't bear it.

In the midst of the conflict, I tried to do the right thing as a leader. I tried to manage each situation and stand up to harmful behavior when necessary. But I was also overwhelmed by it all, and in my struggle and pain, I tightened my grip too much. There were moments when I even began to break bad, to engage in my own empire business, my own unhealthy institutionalism. While I didn't want to control *people*, I desperately wanted to control the *situation* and keep the dream—this church!—alive. I became deeply frustrated, listened to bad advice, and made some rash decisions out of my own pain. I should have backed off and made space for God to work. I should have just let go. But instead, like a bad winter driver, my anxious attempts to steer out of the skid only made it more inevitable that we'd end up in a ditch.

There was a point toward the end, though, when things calmed down and peace returned and it seemed we might be getting a chance to "replant" the church. I attempted to cast a vision for how we might learn from the season of conflict and continue in faithful and fruitful ministry over the longer haul. Despite the deep anxiety I still felt, it was a strangely hopeful moment, an opportunity to redeem the challenges we'd faced and grow into a more mature kingdom presence in our city.

But something else was coming that became my undoing.

⬧　　⬧　　⬧

There is another scene in *Breaking Bad* that has become nothing less than iconic. In it, Walter's wife, Skyler, urges her husband to stop his illicit activities and turn himself in to the police before it's too late. She is worried about what might happen if one of Walt's drug cartel enemies ever shows up at the door.

But she doesn't understand who he has become. He is not her husband, not the same man, not anymore. He is Heisenberg, a drug lord obsessed with power and control, a man consumed by the business of empire.

He turns and growls, "I am not in danger, Skyler. I *am* the danger. A guy opens this door and gets shot and you think that of me? No. *I am the one who knocks.*"

And soon enough, he was showing up at my door.

●　　●　　●

My efforts to lead our group in a replanting process were well intentioned and even well thought out. But they were an illusion. Because another reality was waiting to erupt, a reality whose day had come.

I'd been getting nothing but encouragement from my father, convincing me even more that we had turned a corner and left the bishoping days far behind us. But as we entered the final few months of the church's life, his support for me vanished. It was replaced by aggression, actions he had always used to diminish and control me. My theology was now unacceptable; I was horribly unspiritual; I was deficient, incapable, not enough; I needed to step aside and let him take over. He saw his opportunity and seized it. When I was at my most vulnerable, instead of encouraging my wife and me, instead of honoring the good work we had done and helping us complete it, instead of seeking our restoration and well being, he sought to push me out and cast me aside. Privately, he treated me with contempt; publicly, he undermined what was left of my leadership. He told lies to and about me. He worked to establish as much of his own influence as he could in what remained of our group while subverting any influence that I had left.

Even though I had always been hesitant about his involvement and should have seen this coming, it threw me for a loop. Who would do this to their own son—*again?* This wasn't punishment that fit any crime; this was just the same old dividing pattern rearing its ugly head. I spent hours agonizing in prayer trying to figure out what to do next. I still didn't want this relationship to be ruined, but how could it survive if he was intent on ruining me?

I knew, as his actions unfolded, that there was no way to salvage our church. It was now unhealthy at the root. It was time to let go, to accept the death that needed to come. My desire became to bring things to an end as carefully and peacefully as possible, so that the people who remained in our ragged little congregation—people I deeply loved—could transition to a new church or at least a new season of life. But as I attempted to do that, my father saw his opportunity to be in control slipping away.

In an attempt to retaliate and assert his dominance, my father led a calculated final attack that viciously targeted my wife, our marriage, and our calling. He bishoped my soul into the ground one last time, refusing to hear any of the truth from me, satisfied to do whatever he could to harm me in the final moments. I could hardly believe what was happening. I was undone. His rejection of me as a person, as a son, and, now, as a leader was complete.

Like Brother Dawson, the radical man he had followed all those years, my father had become the one who knocks. And here I was, a grown man with children, pastoring a church out of my own calling, still on the other side of his gun.

I was caught up in a full-scale eruption of the real, my very own apocalypse. It was the kind of revealing that burned the eyes, that stripped out every illusion. Everything I had worked for, everything I had believed in, was shattering right before my eyes. I had given my life to this church, spent everything to see it through. There was nothing left to give.

Jesus prayed that the Father would make us, his church, one, free from the schisms wrought by pathological ambition, empire building, authoritarian control.* But after this eruption, the only demographic I could see myself belonging to, the only group I could be one with, was the dones.

---

* John 17.

Part 2

Darkness
and
Deconstruction

Chapter 6

Roll Credits
(On the First Half of Life)

At this point, it might be helpful to note that the doctrine my family embodied for all those years, which reared its ugly head again in those final moments of my church-planting experience, is not the reality of all American Christianity. It is, as I've mentioned, the reality of authoritarian control.

I include this part of my story for two reasons. One, I know that many, to greater or lesser degrees, have experienced the devastation caused by authoritarian Christianity. And this experience leads them to conclude that either the church or the faith is fundamentally dehumanizing and bankrupt and that there is no healthy reason to continue in it. I want to say "me too" and to argue against telling those who have survived such things to "get over it." The status quo illusion is so glaringly offensive because it is incapable of empathy toward those who have suffered this kind of trauma and loss.

And two, speaking the reality of such experiences is not irrelevant to the many who have never experienced such things. The common rebuttal to stories of trauma or abuse in the church is that these are exceptions, bound to produce disgruntled believers or ex-believers, but irrelevant to the discussion of larger issues, like doctrine, belief, and practice or the phenomenon of religious decline. They'd say that these experiences color people's perspectives so that they don't see clearly. But I think the opposite is often true: experiences of severe Christian authoritarianism or abuse can, when there has been significant time to process them, produce a sharper eye for the ways empire business is harming the church.

When John the Revelator laid into the Laodicean church, I'm sure it was quite a shock to them. Their church was healthy, darn it! Because of the size and strength and sustainability of this community, they likely took great issue with a "hater" like John. How dare he criticize when God was so clearly blessing this Laodicean movement. Look at how much good they were accomplishing. Look at how many people had come to faith through their ministry.

But when one considers, for instance, the destroyed faith of someone sexually abused by a priest or pastor, it would be the height of arrogance to shame them by labeling their experience an unfortunate exception, overshadowed by all the good the institution is doing. Instead, such a tragedy must be viewed as an opportunity for humility, for rooting out the systemic realities that enabled it to take place. (This is, of course, what the Roman Catholic Church famously and meticulously avoided doing until global eruptions of the real overtook it.) At the theological and structural levels, there are all manner of problems with authority, power, and control begging for reformation. And so much more so as the culture shifts beneath our feet, shaking structures of authority.

It also would be helpful for me to say that this is not, I believe, the end of the story. While I know that the grace of God envelops in beloved embrace all those who have suffered at the hands of the church, whether or not they go on believing, I also know that this great revealing is leading us to a hopeful and brilliant new beginning. And the hardship of this decline in the American church is an opportunity for healing and reformation. As long as broken and sinful human beings are involved, we are never going to arrive at perfection, but there is hope that, regardless of the numbers—successful or failing, growing or shrinking—the roots of Jesus-centered humility might grow again to produce the fruit of love and justice, however imperfectly.

I have to believe that our apocalyptic moment, revealing, as it is, who we really are and who Jesus really is, provides us with a powerful occasion to reflect on Jesus' deepest desire for his church, which he expressed in his intercessory prayer in John 17:20–23: "My prayer is not for them alone. I pray also for those who will believe in me through their message, that all of them may be one, Father, just as you are in me and I am in you. May they also be in us so that the world may believe that you have sent me. I have given them the glory that you gave me, that they may be one as we are one—I in them and you in me—so that they may be brought to complete unity. Then the world will know that you sent me and have loved them even as you have loved me."

As impossible as these words seemed when I reached the point of being done, I now find in them the assurance that this apocalypse is not the end of my story either.

Eruption, Unfolding

The eruption of the real and the destruction of all of my illusions at the end of our church plant had both initial and ongoing effects. It had come upon me suddenly, as a thief in the night, catching me unaware. But its ramifications unfolded slowly and painfully over the next few years.

Despite the sudden blast, it took a lot of time to clear away the darkness that had descended over my life. It was a gradual, painstaking kind of work. A process that took the shape of the apostle's words in Ephesians 5:

> But everything exposed by the light becomes visible—and everything that is illuminated becomes a light. This is why it is said:
>
> > "Wake up, sleeper,
> > rise from the dead,
> > and Christ will shine on you."*

I had come to my own place of death. But I wanted so desperately to wake up from my sleep, to rise.

I wanted a reason—any reason—to believe that the light could still win, even in the midst of so much darkness.

* * *

When Kalen and I decided to start the church, we were certain the Lord had called us to do it. We even felt that God had spoken to us through pastor and author Tim Keller at a conference where we saw him speak. His exhortation was for people like us, hesitant, on-the-cusp church-planters. He gave us permission

---

* Verses 13–14.

to follow God's call regardless of obstacles and naysayers, which seemed like a message from the Spirit to give us the push we needed to move forward with one heart and mind. So we felt a spiritual kind of confidence, a confidence that seemed repeatedly confirmed when God provided last-minute funds to make rent on our meeting space, or brought peace out of a conflict or disagreement, or worked through the church's ministry to accomplish something beautiful for the kingdom. Even if we could have envisioned the church coming to an end, we most certainly could not have envisioned the kind of unraveling we experienced, with such hurtful behavior from trusted people and with such painful relational fracture, the cracks of which seemed to spiderweb in all directions.

But it goes deeper than that. Calling is not a word I throw around to describe a casual sense of talent or a desired vocation (which is a popular usage); I use it to describe a deeply ingrained sense that my life was always supposed to be dedicated to ministry in Jesus' church. That sense of calling got me through so much. There has virtually never been a time in my life, especially not since adolescence, when I was not ministering or preparing to minister in some way. And I believed deep in my bones that this church I was finally stepping out to start with my wife was the culmination of that lifetime journey.

I remember a time way back in Miami when my father had been especially excited about the "fivefold ministry" of Ephesians 4, which was central to the notion of restoring the end-times apostles and prophets, something he had undoubtedly picked up from Brother Dawson's book and tapes. He was on about it constantly, and he decided it was time to see where his firstborn son fit. In case you don't know, the five ministry gifts listed by the apostle Paul in Ephesians 4 are apostle, prophet, evangelist, pastor, and teacher. And my father thought I clearly demonstrated the gifting of an apostle *and* an evangelist—even at seven or eight years old, or whatever I was at the time.

I don't think there was much to indicate such a gifting at that point. But for some reason, I've always gone back to that moment of "naming." My father even commemorated it with a pair of dog tags that he got engraved at the mall. (It was the '80s.) And there it was, a militant designation of my ministry fit, my lifetime mission, engraved in metal and hanging from my chubby little neck: Zach Hoag, Apostle-Evangelist.

So maybe it makes a little more sense that I couldn't have foreseen it all going down the way it did.

At first, this ending was so overwhelming that the only conclusion I could consider was that the spiritual premise I started with, wrapped up as it was in beliefs about God, about Jesus, about the church, about my identity and calling, about community and relationships and family, was flawed. I became convinced that my calling, dog tags and all, must be a sham.

After the church closure was complete, I remember tweeting, "Everything changes."

And that tweet was about as prophetic as it could possibly be.

This Is (the Rest of) Your Life

Franciscan priest Father Richard Rohr has taught extensively about the transition from the first half of life to the second. But in Rohr's teaching, this transition doesn't just have to do with age: "When I say that you will enter the second half of life, I don't mean it in a strictly chronological way. Some young people, especially those who have learned from early suffering, are already there, and some older folks are still quite childish."[1]

This transition has to do with suffering, whether self-inflicted or otherwise. It has to do with failing and falling in an epic, life-changing fashion. And it has to do with a death. An emotional and spiritual death. A death to the ego. This is why not everyone makes the transition to discover a deeper way of spiritual living. They do everything they can to avoid the pain of that death. In Father Rohr's words, "The human ego prefers anything, just about anything, to falling or changing or dying. The ego is that part of you that loves the status quo, even when it is not working."[2]

The ego, in this sense, is not always a particular kind of personality or character trait. It is rather a deep-seated force that drives us in the first half of life. The ego is concerned with appearances, with accomplishments, with achieving a level of status or success. And the ego hates to lose, can't bear the thought of suffering or changing. Thus it was my ego and even my own empire business that drove me to cling so hard and become so anxious and fearful as our church plant unraveled. It was my ego that drove me to hold on for dear life and prolong something that was no longer working. It was my ego that became entangled with my lifelong sense of calling, such that I couldn't bear the thought of failure or loss, couldn't just let go and trust God's unfolding work.

And so it was my dying ego that internalized a deep level of humiliation and shame from the ending of all I had worked for, and from the piercing hurts and offenses that followed. In the throes of death, it was my gasping ego that struggled to retain some of its former glory. As gossip spread about our church closure and friends ran for the hills and my calling screeched to halt; as finances dried up and stacks of applications were filled out and no second interviews were scheduled; as the way I had been living and moving and operating in what was essentially my hometown underwent such a radical transformation that it seemed my place in the world had vanished overnight; during all of this painful aftermath, it was my ego that was writhing toward its end. No suffering does this ego-killing job quite like becoming a scapegoat in your community, a failure branded with a scarlet F.

I tried desperately to retain some shred of my identity as a pastor, a leader, a minister, something. To keep that lifelong calling intact. To don those dog tags, even though the scarlet F had become my new accessory. To somehow prove myself to that network that was disposing of me. But that too was an illusion.

Undergoing this ego death, and clearing away the darkness that surrounds it, is a process. While the fatal blow had been struck, it had stages, like grieving always does. And those stages represented a gradual acceptance of the truth, a progressive shedding of illusions and denials.

It took weeks, months, years even, to see that the status quo of my life was no longer working. It was a brutal process of facing my pain over and over again, feeling those terrible feelings and feeling them to the full. It entailed fully coming to terms for the first time with my authoritarian upbringing. It meant that everything was up for grabs, including my anger and resentment toward anyone who wronged me. It meant an openness to the future, rather than a fearful, closed-off existence. And eventually it led to nothing less than my transformation, and the transformation of my precious little family.

In his writing on the subject, Father Rohr makes an interesting move from the personal dimension of this "further journey" to a cultural and ecclesial one too. He envisions both the culture and the church as fixated on first-half-of-life issues: "We are a 'first-half-of-life culture,' largely concerned about surviving successfully . . . Our institutions and our expectations, including our churches, are almost entirely configured to encourage, support, reward, and validate the tasks of the first half of life. Shocking and disappointing, but I think it is true."[3]

Elsewhere, he talks about those who are caught up in "early stage religion," which is fixated on "maintaining order and social control."[4] And this is where we might ask ourselves whether American Christianity's apocalyptic moment is really a transition from the first half of life to the second. Is it a gracious opportunity to put off more of its ego and discover more of its soul? Could this great revealing be ushering in a great ending to "anything that justifies the status quo,"[5] so that American Christians might move on to maturity and deeper, fuller, more abundant life, a genuine new beginning?

•   •   •

Here's a bit more of the context of Ephesians 4:

> So Christ himself gave the apostles, the prophets, the evangelists, the pastors and teachers, to equip his people for works of service, so that the body of Christ may be built up until we all reach unity in the faith and in the knowledge of the Son of God and *become mature, attaining to the whole measure of the fullness of Christ.*
>
> Then we will no longer be infants, tossed back and forth by the waves, and blown here and there by every wind of

teaching and by the cunning and craftiness of people in their deceitful scheming. Instead, speaking the truth in love, *we will grow to become in every respect the mature body of him who is the head, that is, Christ.* From him the whole body, joined and held together by every supporting ligament, grows and builds itself up in love, as each part does its work.

—*verses 11–16, emphases mine*

The purpose of this passage, and the purpose of these fivefold ministry gifts, is to aid the church in becoming mature in every respect. It is most certainly not about a grandiose end-times vision in which superleaders with superauthority operate with near-superpowers and exercise superdominion. That's ego nonsense. And it is not even about what I once thought of my own calling; this apocalypse has finally revealed the immaturity wrapped up in that old drive to have a church-ministry identity. The rigid grip on this calling can quickly become an ego-driven illusion, what the Bible might call an idol. It's the stuff of the first half of life, not the stuff of "attaining to the full measure of Christ." And part of the reason I held so tightly to the vision of our church plant in the final days, strategizing ways to revive it and control the outcome, becoming anxious in my leadership decisions, is because I was caught up in something that lacked the trajectory, or *telos,* of what Paul envisions here. We had yet to transition, yet to make the "further journey," and the result was that we were, in the end, "tossed back and forth by the waves."

The other critical point is that these fivefold leadership gifts are oriented toward equipping, which divests them of authoritarianism. The apostles, prophets, evangelists, pastors, and teachers exist to equip God's people to do their own works of service! All of the members of Christ's body possess their own spiritual gifts, as we all share in the "one Spirit" (v. 4) who has given gifts to each one of us (cf. 1 Corinthians 12). New Testament scholar N. T. Wright adds this: "Sometimes when the church debates the nature of different offices and ministries, you get the impression that these things exist for their own sake, as though the main point of there being a church in the first place was that certain people would be 'special' within it. The opposite is the case. The main point of certain people having special roles is so that every single Christian, and the church as a whole, may be equipped for their work of service."[6]

This little passage that played such a huge role in my upbringing, and in my perspective on myself and my calling, is pregnant with the potential for a great ending, because the empire business that so often infects Christian faith in America is demolished by the notion that the purpose of leadership in the church is to call *the people* into maturity by equipping *the people* for service in their own lives, in their own neighborhoods, according to their own gifts. And while this is a genuine, foundational kind of leadership in the church that brings order and direction, its purpose is never mere social control to perpetuate the status quo. Because that's just early stage religion.

In the next few chapters, I'll dig a little more into the process that began when our church plant ended. It's a process marked not only by darkness but also by deconstruction. The "necessary suffering" Rohr talks about is deconstructive by nature. But it is not a safe endeavor. It's a process one must push through and never simply get stuck in. Because on the other side is resurrection, light. On the other side is the rest of your one, abundant gift of life.*

---

* John 10:10.

Maybe you have also experienced some of this "necessary suffering" in your life, the kind of suffering where everything changes, and maybe it has shaken you to the core of your identity and calling. If so, you are not alone.

And on a much larger scale, it just may be that the decline of American Christianity is a bit of necessary suffering too, a great ending to the status quo and a death to our collective ego.

One can only guess at what lies beyond.

One can only hope for the beauty that might come after.

Chapter 7

The Desert of Deconstruction

I sat down at my desk in the office room that would soon be taken over by my one-year-old's crib. I'd been coming here a lot, usually late at night, to write—specifically, to blog.

And that night I wrote a barnburner of a blog post, the kind where hitting "publish" is a nervous kind of thrill, an adrenaline high. Blogging can be like an extreme sport for tired, homebound dads, especially homebound dads whose lives have recently fallen apart.

•　　•　　•

I've always been a writer, and I've got stacks of childhood journals and notebooks to prove it. Ever since those days when I first got access to the internet, I've been putting words online—engaging in lengthy debates on Calvinist message boards, writing Reformed theology articles (that no one read) for a website I cobbled together, posting prosaic spiritual statuses to Myspace. While church planting, I kept a low-key blog that was read mostly by church members and local folks and maybe shared a few times outside of those circles. And our church was very tech-savvy for the time, so I took on the role of creating content for our church website and social media accounts too. This was on top of the routine of sermon preparation—week after week composing my talks manuscript-style, delivering them almost verbatim on Sunday, then promptly posting them to our church podcast.

During the last year of the church, I had the opportunity to write a book with a small publisher—a pop-culture and theology mashup called *Nothing but the Blood: The Gospel according to Dexter*. That book became a sort of pastoral memoir, drawing on nearly four years of sermon series and recounting my experiences as a church planter, with all of my hard-won ideas about what it means to be the church in these transitional times. Of course, by the time the manuscript was finished, things had gone from challenging to alarming in our church plant. And by the time the book released, the church was already closed, rendering most of the book's hopeful conclusions quite nearly moot. Even the bio on the back cover was an out-and-out lie: "He serves as lead pastor."

Not only was I not a lead pastor anymore, but the final fracturing of the church had left me with virtually no one to celebrate the book release with. And not much reason to celebrate anyway.

So I found myself blogging because I wanted to continue living out my passion for writing, and to at least find some way to build on the sorrowful release of my book. But also I was just desperate to tell my story. I had an almost visceral urge to process through writing. And that this processing was happening in public meant that I might receive something else I desperately longed for: a "me too."

The barnburner of a blog post I wrote that night was born in the primordial ooze of my grief and depression. It was a searing critique of what I still very much believe to be a harmful church trend—the newer iteration of the old Pentecostal prosperity gospel, which I creatively labeled "celebrity Christianity" for its preoccupation with mimicking American celebrity culture. But the accusatory tone and caustic delivery were sharpened by my own sharp pain. And the next morning, the me-toos and attaboys came raining down. It was online validation substituting for healing, for now. If I was not yet giving in to cynicism, I was only a few more posts and shares and comments away from it.

In the following weeks and months, I continued to fight at the keyboard, processing my story while trying to retain some semblance of my pastoral identity. I was in the throes of deconstruction. And the more critical my blog posts became, the more cynical I began to feel. It sometimes felt like I was holding onto my cynicism like a lifeline.

The Desert of the Real

It was 1999, nearly a decade before I ever considered planting a church, and American culture was bracing itself for the almost certain technological disaster of Y2K. On Easter weekend of that year, I happened to be on a road trip to Ohio with a few friends to, of all things, act as a judge for a rollerblading competition. So you can see that on several levels, I was truly standing in the precarious liminal space between the crazy '90s and the incoming millennium.

And let me add one other thing to the mix: on that road trip, my friends and I went to see a movie, the 1999 sci-fi blockbuster *The Matrix*.

I mentioned earlier that while I don't truly belong to generation X, I'm not quite a millennial either. And nowhere are my generation Y bona fides more clearly on display than on this pre-Y2K road trip. To this day, *The Matrix* tops my list of most influential movies.

This odd, proto-digital-age, sci-fi-meets-classic-kung-fu romp that dominated box offices that year also became a sermon-illustration favorite for gen Xers and gen Yers. None of my friends who saw the movie with me that day were Christians. And since it was Easter weekend, I came out of the theater feeling like my eyes had been opened and my faith had been confirmed and I simply had to start evangelizing right then and there in the car ride back to the hotel room. I couldn't stop going on and on about how "this movie is everything I truly believe," which probably made them quite nervous that my religion amounted to a green-tinted glorification of geeks and goths. But that didn't matter, because I was experiencing something like a mini resurrection and couldn't stop preaching "Jesus is Neo!" sermons to my buddies for days afterward.

Now, however, the significance of this film for me goes beyond those initial feelings and symbolic parallels. It even goes beyond the prescient tech vision of the Wachowskis, in which hackers, coders, and programmers are heroes and saviors and the key to everything, which is the cultural narrative we now inhabit, the digital age giving way to something like Silicon Valley world domination. No, the ongoing significance for me now is found in something more subtle, something in the background of the film: its profound vision of reality. I think that's what really hit me deep down when I first saw it too, mired as I still was in spiritual homelessness, the brokenness of my background, the search for belonging, and not yet having reached the moment of my apocalypse and its eruptions of the real.

It's been widely reported that each cast member of the film was required to read French philosopher Jean Baudrillard's *Simulacra and Simulation*. The physical book even makes a cameo in an early scene, and you might have missed the moment when the character Morpheus quotes Baudrillard. Standing with the newly awakened Neo in a computer-training program, Morpheus surveys what has become of the world, the world Neo has never actually seen. He says, "Welcome to the desert of the real."[1]

In Baudrillard's book, the phrase appears in this context: "It is the real, and not the map, whose vestiges persist here and there in the deserts that are no longer those of the Empire, but ours. The desert of the real itself."[2]

In chapter 1 I briefly introduced political philosopher Slavoj Zizek, who talked about ideology and the real. Zizek borrowed the phrase "the real" from Baudrillard, and it became the title of his book *Welcome to the Desert of the Real*. Both of these philosophers can be at least generally linked to the tradition of postmodern deconstructionism, which is all about questioning the structure of how we understand reality (including all manifestations of authority), and identifying the illusions that we embrace to keep our lives going. While postmodernism and deconstruction both often get a bad rap in Christian circles, I believe there is something in deconstructive thought that is essential to authentic Christian faith. If we are not willing to question the realities of our faith and practice, or face the real when it erupts in our life of faith, we'll stay forever stuck in early stage religion.

Deconstruction is a necessary work that brings us to our necessary ending so that we can find our way through to a new beginning.

• • •

While *The Matrix* is at the top of my movie list, my top TV show is another deconstructionist masterpiece: *Mad Men*.

Mad Men is about as different in form and content from the geeky tech epic as anything could possibly be. But at its core is a similar deconstructive message. And it is, at least to my mind, not just the best TV show of this revolutionary TV era but the best TV show ever—in the traditional, week-by-week, serial-storytelling form. And that's because it is a throwback to that form, a gradually unfolding 1960s period melodrama that patiently develops the plot lines for each character while paying unrivaled attention to detail in costume, backdrop, and dialogue. The performances are at once restrained and profound, with a depth not seen in other shows. The commitment to realism is rigorous. And its realistic central character, Don Draper, is now, like Walter White, nothing less than a cultural icon.

Don Draper is the quintessential 1960s ad man, and *Mad Men* tells the story of the advent of the advertising industry on Madison Avenue. This is the moment in our nation's history when our materialistic fates were sealed. We became a people defined by material things, things meant to make our lives easier or more fun, produced in mass quantities to feed an insatiable cultural appetite. And that appetite was fueled by advertising.

Early on in the series, Don describes the goal of advertising as selling happiness. In the boardroom, Don repeatedly does exactly that, creating scenarios that attach emotional, if not transcendental, value to otherwise common products and services—cigarettes, women's stockings, vacuum cleaners. He brings his clients to tears or laughter or both, and opens their wallets besides. Deals are closed, Clio Awards are won.

The ad man not only sells happiness, he becomes a millionaire.

But anyone who has watched the show also knows that the ad man is a fraud, living with a stolen identity to hide an act of cowardice. And this is where *Mad Men*'s deconstructive spirit manifests. Because those colorful dresses and sharp suits cannot hide the fact that the era in our nation's history when the current culture of out-of-control consumerism was born was built on a lie, just like Don's life was built on a lie—the lie that we are defined by things, that we derive meaning and value from what we consume, that in seeking success we will somehow find our true selves.

The lie that our blessedness and belovedness can be calculated by material gains.

The lie that we can love God (or self or others) truly *and* love money too.

The lie that the economics of ego will offer us any answers.

The lie that happiness is bought and sold.

* * *

The deconstructive season that began when our church plant ended seemed to bring up so many of the themes I'd struggled with since my adolescence. All the things that didn't add up. All the inconsistencies, hypocrisies, and lies.

Like some of the ways I witnessed leaders mixing Jesus and money.

All the way back at that Texas cult, I learned that mixing Jesus and money could go very wrong. Brother Dawson was a longtime student of the charismatic word-of-faith teaching, the kind where you believe it and receive it; name it and claim it; confess the promises of God, sow financial seeds of faith, and reap a harvest of health and wealth. He apprenticed with one of the early pioneers of that movement. The church in East Texas was therefore deeply rooted in prosperity gospel soil, even as it had grown into its unique Latter Rain/Manifest Sons of God authoritarianism. Brother Dawson's vision of the last days apostles and prophets exercising untold spiritual power and dominion relied heavily on the formula of verbally asserting the promises of God and expecting supernatural results. And the empire business of the East Texas church was not without an economic dimension.

The way this worked out was pretty simple. The discipleship demanded by Brother Dawson and the elders required that one's resources were not to be considered one's own. Making an honest living for your family's health and flourishing was a fleshly and selfish pursuit. Your money belonged to "the house." It belonged to your true family—those who do the will of God, those who are part of this ultimate move of God. It belonged to the leadership of the Jasper church.

The congregation thus gave of their finances with abandon, despite the fact that most folks faced serious financial hardship. They gave to support the church as it plotted large-scale church and residential expansion (which never came to fruition), and they gave to maintain Brother Dawson's enormous ranch (which functioned as his personal prophetic mountaintop and an untouchable revelatory retreat center for the church elite). They gave believing that they would receive a hundredfold return, a miraculous kind of happiness manifested in both this great big spiritual family in Jasper, and great big financial blessings (that would enable them to bless their true family all the more). At one pivotal point in the cult's history, people gave stacks of money to an investment scheme Brother Dawson claimed to receive from God by direct revelation, a scheme revolving around purebred show horses to be raised and sold at the ranch.

As bizarre as that all may sound, the people of the Jasper church were primed for such a proposition. And they took it as a prophetic word from the Lord that would guarantee a return on this investment that would, they believed, enrich their leader, enrich them, and enrich the church as it launched even farther into its destiny of power and dominion leading up to the end.

What happened instead is that numerous families, many of them already living at the poverty line in an economically dry little Texas town, were cheated in a fundamentally untenable—and probably illegal—scheme. Some lost homes, their life savings, everything.

Brother Dawson sold happiness, and Brother Dawson was a fraud.

But that wasn't the last time I ran into mad money religion in a charismatic context. Several years later, after we had left the church in East Texas, my family traveled to see a favorite author and speaker at a megachurch in Indiana. This speaker was known for having a prophetic edge in the charismatic world, calling Spirit-filled folks like us to ditch the trappings of worldliness and immorality and get back to wholehearted following after Jesus. His message was often a heavyhanded one, coming down hard on the casual "churchianity" that would rather have fun programs, ear-tickling sermons, and an easy life than genuine spiritual awakening and revival, because revival requires holiness, and awakening won't happen if Christians are lukewarm.

His message resonated with me in my spiritual searching, as I was already becoming disillusioned with the flaky charismatics of my youth and especially their prosperity gospel. But this speaker, like so many, missed the essential ingredient of John the Revelator's diatribe against Laodicean lukewarmness. And I was about to see that on glaring display.

His sermon that day had been another full-throated condemnation of the church's unholiness, lukewarmness, and easy churchianity. Immediately afterward, I happened to walk out the wrong door of the massive church building to a hidden part of the parking lot. There were about fifteen parking spaces adjacent to the building and several more under a carport. The pastor of this particular megachurch was out there, along with other church leaders and the guest speaker we had traveled such a long way to see. The only cars present (and, I assume, allowed) on this lot were brand-new luxury vehicles—Cadillacs, Suburbans, Porsches—gleaming in the sun as if on display at a dealership. All the leaders laughed and joked before piling in and speeding off, and I knew I was seeing something I wasn't supposed to see—at least not like that.

It was a glimpse behind the curtain, the vehicles a stark contrast with the old minivans and sedans all the families like mine had unloaded hours earlier. And while I'm sure he was somehow able to rationalize this even in the midst of his tirades against lukewarmness, I simply couldn't. In my mind, *this* was lukewarmness. It was a contradiction. I had just been subjected to a bombastic message about my desperately lacking holiness from the same man who was now departing from a secret lot like royalty or some sort of celebrity.

There was also the time in Arizona some years after that, during the trip on which I had my pivotal encounter with my father in a different kind of parking lot. Days earlier, at yet another charismatic megachurch, I shifted uncomfortably in my seat as the world-famous pastor mounted the stage to preach a sermon based on his recently released book. This was toward the beginning of my Calvinist phase, and my distaste for health-and-wealth flakiness was at an all-time high. I was *this* close to abandoning charismatic Christianity. Yet here I was, sitting in the natural habitat of the prosperity gospel, listening to as baldfaced a name-it-and-claim-it, health-and-wealth sales pitch as I'd ever heard.

The premise was simple: God promises to bless us with as much money as possible, both for our wealth and enjoyment and so that we can give more to the kingdom. That was problematic enough, but it wasn't the worst of it. The worst was when this famous pastor launched into a riff about how he and his wife would be spending part of the next leg of his tour shopping on Rodeo Drive. This was offered in protest to those who "don't think Christian leaders should walk in prosperity."

"But I'm going to walk in the blessing of God, and I'm going to bless my wife with the best! And you should too!" His voice crescendoed and the sanctuary erupted in amens and applause. The world-famous worship team that was traveling with him was cued and the offering was collected as people who would never be able to afford a shopping spree on Rodeo Drive emptied their wallets.

We might as well have been in Don Draper's boardroom.

The Economics of Ego

The good work of deconstruction that facilitates a necessary ending in our life of faith will often make use of capable critique.

It will confront abuses and dismantle inconsistencies. Both on a personal or heart level and, in the church community, on a corporate or cultural level, deconstruction pulls down the strongholds of empire business, sometimes razing them right to the ground. And during my season of darkness and deconstruction, after the death of my dream and the bleeding out of my ego, I pulled my chair up to the blue screen night after night to see what manner of empire business I could deconstruct, one keystroke at a time.

But deconstruction can leave us open to cynicism. Deconstructive critique and hardening cynicism are not synonymous, nor does the first automatically lead to the second. But during this season, I experienced how easy it is to make this unfortunate step. I am glad that God was patient and loving with me, working even in the midst of that darkness. And if you think you have slipped from the good but difficult deconstructive space into a cynical space, know that God is patient and loving with you too.

And there's a better way ahead, if you keep pushing through.

•   •   •

It might be tempting to assign all of the American church's economic problems to the prosperity-gospel charismatics I encountered at various points in my life; they present an obvious target. But if anything, the word-of-faith teaching epitomized by Brother Dawson merely reflects the values of American consumer culture. Those values are just translated into a Christian context: that we measure the blessing of God on ourselves and our churches in terms of up-and-to-the-right financials, popular and prosperous leaders, and standing-room-only Sunday services.

If institutionalism practices exclusion to insure the institution's survival, then what we have in the economic dimension of empire business is consumerism. And when we locate the root there, we can see that this way of the empire impacts all of us, even at the deepest level of our hearts.

In chapter 1 I mentioned a missiologist from Canada who identified one cause in the shift to a post-Christian culture as the laissez-faire capitalism that we have almost all embraced. It is the air we breathe, even within the church. And I would venture to guess that the *Mad Men* 1960s were a trendsetting decade that shaped American culture, including American Christianity, in this regard. The church has, in one way or another, been prone to selling happiness ever since. We have assumed the role of distributor of goods and services, hoping our products—church buildings, Sunday services, worship bands, niche programs—can attract enough of the right people. It's an economic endeavor, even if money isn't the main motivator; we are trying to draw in consumers with the products we're advertising. And the result is an individualism (what benefit can *I* derive from this?) and a passivity (I'm here to watch, experience, ingest) rather than a collectivism (this is about us, not me) and a worshipful mission (I'm here to worship God and then join the work). We also hope folks pay for their individual experience.

The decline of Christian faith in the US offers us a vital opportunity to face this consumer reality. I believe this aspect of the American church's empire business is actually hastening our necessary ending.

Perhaps another way of approaching this is to address relevance as a primary concern among Christians and churches today. When we were planting our church, this was top of mind for us: how could we do something that was relevant to the people and the culture we wanted to reach? As I mentioned earlier, I really thought my skinny jeans and American Apparel hoodie were important parts of the mission. I was being myself as a person in, and not removed from, the culture. Church shouldn't be something other; it should be something among.

And while there is something good about seeking to be among the culture you are ministering to, there is a pitfall here too. And it is primarily about consumerism. Relevance can become an ideology, an illusion that may create surface success but won't sustain us and help us weather storms like the decline that is raging right now. It may put a bandage on things or boost attendance for a while, but the deeper gospel impact of engaging true worshipers of Jesus and committed workers for God's mission and his justice in the world will fail to take root.

So when I pulled up my chair to write a scathing blog post about this new prosperity-gospel trend that I labeled celebrity Christianity, I was at least getting something right—the heart of the matter, if not the method. It was a necessary dismantling. In this popular manifestation of empire business, the leaders seek to set the tone for everyone else by living a lavish celebrity lifestyle, complete with famous friends, expensive designer labels, and dynamic bands producing chart-topping albums. But their efforts fail to produce the justice of God, which always lifts up those oppressed by the upper echelons of wealth. Their efforts fail to be good news for the poor, including the poor and oppressed sitting in the seats of those very churches.

And what about God's justice rolling on like a river?* What about the economic equality of the kingdom of God, where all is

---

* Amos 5:24.

shared so no one lacks what they need?* What about the biblical command to modesty (which, contextually, is a commentary on the expense of the clothing on display rather than how much skin they cover)?†

In our consumeristic milieu, we desperately need the deconstructive critique Jesus applied to the rich young ruler, whose "great wealth" was the barrier to his comprehending and partaking in the kingdom. And we desperately need John the Revelator's lesson to the Laodiceans, whose lukewarm sickness was specifically in their believing "I have acquired wealth and do not need a thing."‡

As Father Rohr reminds us, "Many have opted for the soft religion of easy ego consolations, the human growth model, or the 'prosperity Gospel' that has become so common in Western Christianity and in all the worlds we spiritually colonize. We do grow and increase, but by a far different path than the ego would ever imagine. Only the soul knows and understands."[3]

The ego economics of empire must be deconstructed, especially as they impact how we do Christianity in the US. It's much bigger than a little celebrity Christianity trend, far more sweeping. And we must look to prophetic voices who are doing such deconstructive work well. Voices like Pope Francis, who said this in his 2013 *Evangelii Gaudium* ("Joy of the Gospel"): "Just as the commandment 'Thou shalt not kill' sets a clear limit in order to safeguard the value of human life, today we also have to say 'thou shalt not' to an economy of exclusion and inequality. Such an economy kills." And "some people continue to defend

---

* Acts 2:42ff.
† 1 Timothy 2:9.
‡ Revelation 3:17.

the trickle-down theories which assume that economic growth, encouraged by a free market, will inevitably succeed in bringing about greater justice and inclusiveness in the world. This opinion, which has never been confirmed by the facts, expresses a crude and naive trust in the goodness of those wielding economic power and in the sacralized workings of the prevailing economic system. Meanwhile, the excluded are still waiting."[4]

Sometimes the powerful deconstructive truth comes from an unexpected prophet, like Garrison Keillor, former host of NPR's *A Prairie Home Companion:*

> The evangelicals who brought me up . . . avoided money-grubbing. They were above that . . . Those evangelicals are still around, studying the Word, doing good and living modestly, and they are writhing in discomfort at the carryings-on of the Rolex Christians and their gospel of prosperity. And their shamelessness . . .
>
> For me, what works is high Anglican, a modest rector, not overly jovial like a game show host, an organist who knows his place, and liturgy with some long silences in it. 'Be still, and know that I am God,' He says. So let's. God speaks in the stillness.[5]

And to that folksy eruption of the real, I can only say amen.

●   ●   ●

Perhaps Keillor's remarks present us with as good an opportunity as any to consider what might come after. At a personal level, is there anything that might come after all the deconstruction and the dismantling and the becoming "one with the dones"? On a much larger scale, what can be built after the deconstructive work is accomplished, once we have arrived in the desert of the real? *The Matrix* paints a picture of a battle to be waged (and won) for human freedom and flourishing beyond the apocalypse of Neo's awakening. And *Mad Men*'s narrative is pregnant with the possibility of redemption beyond Don Draper's and Madison Avenue's illusions (and eruptions).

Garrison Keillor's words both hearken back and look forward to a simple and imperfect but pure kind of religion, where there is modest living and doing good and God speaking in the ancient liturgy and in the silence to assuage our spiritual wandering. Can we find home after the dismantling?

Because if nothing comes after, deconstruction has no bottom. And no greater purpose. And no hope.

It's just demolition.

Chapter 8

Exit through the Wilderness

As I look back on the four years of church planting, and the year or so of preparation before that, and, really, leaving the Calvinist Baptist church before that, I realize that I was already swept up in a process. Changes were underway in my perspective on theology and spirituality and ministry long before my season of darkness and deconstruction.

Toward the beginning of that process, I broke with the Gospel-Centered New Calvinism that had dominated my thinking for almost a decade. And throughout the church-planting years, new thoughts about the nature and character of God, the meaning of salvation, the work and mission of the church, and the cultural lines of exclusion in my evangelical context rose to the surface. I was captivated by this process and these new revelations, excited for how they might shape and reshape my ministry to our little church and our beloved city of Burlington.

Our church plant, as cutting edge as it sometimes seemed to be, was firmly located within the evangelical world. And because of that, some of my emerging perspectives made our more conservative core members uneasy, if not upset. It's not that I was trying to fool anyone or be a theological rogue; it's just that I was beginning to see everything differently. And that can pose a problem for folks who want things to stay the same.

More than anything else, I felt a fierce determination to stay on the mission of being a church *for* our progressive, post-Christian city, not merely in a superficial sense of staying relevant but in an increasingly deeper sense of discerning how to do theology in the midst of God's mission in our neighborhood, outside the church walls. Part of that process was deconstructive: identifying some of the ways those of us with churched backgrounds might be building barriers in our theology and practice without even knowing it. I was looking for a way to embody acceptance and inclusion, so that our friends and neighbors might experience God and meet Jesus. I didn't want us to just do superficial outreach or create a program to condescendingly engage "those people." I wanted those people to be our people. I wanted *them* to be *us*.

Despite how things ended, despite the moments of breaking bad, I didn't want to be just another pastor insuring the institution's survival and maintaining social control.

One of the sermon series I preached during the last year of our church was called "Exit through the Wilderness," a survey of the book of Exodus with a nod to the Banksy documentary *Exit through the Gift Shop*, because who brilliantly critiques the empire better than Banksy? A sweeping Exodus theology emerges when we see the Scriptures as a story of God liberating all of creation from the effects of human empire—liberation from both the power and control *out there*, and the power and control tempting our hearts to break bad. Yes, the empire you will always have with you. And prone to wander, Lord, I feel it.

The process of moving from one perspective to another was underway in my life for a long time, accelerating to the moment of impact in the end of our church. And that end laid waste to not only the structures around me but those within me too. I had no idea what wilderness awaited me when I preached about the Israelites being liberated from the Egyptian Empire only to feel lost in the sojourn that followed. I didn't know that my necessary suffering would parallel my preaching, that my ego would have to die even as I identified empire business all around me. I was unaware of how deeply I would soon descend into the desert of the real.

·   ·   ·

In this new season of darkness and deconstruction, it dawned on me. I had planted a church in the first half of life. I had written a book in the first half of life. Despite good intentions and a genuine heart, these things were bound up with the ego, with structures around me and within me that were not fully rooted in reality, because I just wasn't there yet on the journey.

The trajectory that had been set when my family moved to a Texas cult had finally and fully arced to its devastating conclusion. All had been revealed; the broken fragments of my life were now scattered across the floor. And I was staying up late every night, writing my way through the desert, sinking into the cynical quicksand, seeking a way out, finding none.

I hesitate to add a "but" here because you may be in a similar space, or may have been there before. And you know, just like I do, that there really is no "but." The deconstructive process is a total kind of thing, with no easy answers, no quick solutions. When you are no longer under any illusions about God or church or community or calling or family or relationships, you can't just switch gears, pull a U-ey, and head on back to Happytown. You've got to face the pain in its fullness. You've got to feel your way through the darkness. There's no other choice, unless you want to live in denial, unless you want more of the lie.

Gradually, after the closure of our church, I let go of the old identity. I thought maybe I could plant another church, but emotionally, spiritually, and socially, I knew it was impossible. I thought maybe moving could open up a new ministry door, but moving only transplanted the deconstructive process to a new location. I thought perhaps building online community could give me the support and opportunities I needed to shortcut the painful process, but online community became just as difficult and unfulfilling as anything we had in real life. While the deathblow was struck in the last act of our church, I was in the throes of dying all the way. Doors had to be closed; never-agains had to be said.

And what I realized, little by little, is that the entanglement of my identity with my call to ministry was at the root of my reality problem. All through the process of church planting, I operated out of the belief that this venture must succeed or else. Or else all is lost. Or else I'm a failure. Or else my life has no deeper, spiritual purpose. Or else I am worthless. Or else the thing I've been destined for and have committed my whole life to is a lie. Or else my father won't approve of me, accept me, be proud of me. It was attached to me like those dog tags; it was placed on me by all those years of control. That's why, though I never wanted to control people, I desperately needed to control the outcome. I didn't want to believe this dream could die.

But all that this perspective had produced was a life of obligation that had me pursuing approval and acceptance and worth through what I should and must do. As devastating as my father's disapproval and rejection were, it was my seeking his approval in the first place that I had to recognize and abandon. My very own apocalypse was meant to demolish the metrics of spiritual achievement in my life, to deconstruct them to the foundation. If I've learned one thing from being a parent, it's that conditional love is no love at all; and all the conditions I'd embraced for myself—from my father, from the dividing, from American Christianity—were being dismantled piece by piece. It was a brutal kind of mercy.

As much as I was convinced that pursuing my calling was equivalent to living out my deepest purpose in life, it was taking me farther off course from my true self. Pastor and author Jonathan Martin explains how "shipwreck" in our lives is often what it takes to reverse this errant direction:

> Deep living comes out of deep healing, which requires us to go deeply into our pain, mistakes, and failures to find the God who meets us there at the bottom. This is the slow, painful process of soul work. But as we do go further into the process, a whole new way of living is made available to us. Where we once simply ignored all that is in the depths of us, duty and obligation were often the only things that kept us afloat . . . Oftentimes we develop an entire religion out of a system of "shoulds" and "oughts" . . .
>
> Before shipwreck, many people don't have a sense they have actually chosen their own lives . . . [but] wholeness is not possible as long as the life we live is not the life we have chosen all the way down to the bottom.[1]

At the bottom of it all, I was meant to discover my own belovedness. And who I really am.

Through this experience of death, I was meant to finally choose life and start living.

Resurrection People

Empire business has manifestations large and small, but it always infects the roots. Whether it's a family or a church institution or a larger church movement or the church's involvement in national politics, the great revealing exposes the gnarled roots that have given rise to harmful fruit. It's never painless, never enjoyable, always a risk. When you have a reality problem to repent of, it's a bitter pill to swallow.

But it's a pill that will save your life.

The American church cannot be its true self and will never accomplish its gospel mission unless it continually repents of its empire business and stays on the kingdom track. Repentance as an ongoing spiritual practice is one of the most beautiful fruits of an apocalypse in our lives, if we are willing to receive it. Will we participate in this necessary suffering leading us to a necessary ending and a new beginning? Or will we keep delaying the inevitable by holding on to that which is passing away?

The New Testament provides a powerful testimony against American consumerist metrics of spiritual achievement. It claims that not only did the Messiah suffer and die, but he did so as a pattern for his people: "To this you were called, because Christ suffered for you, leaving you an example, that you should follow in his steps."* A necessary suffering leading to a necessary ending.

---

* 1 Peter 2:21.

Death and resurrection are not one-time events but an ongoing way of life that militates against empire building:

- "Whoever wants to be my disciple must deny themselves and take up their cross and follow me. For whoever wants to save their life will lose it, but whoever loses their life for me will find it" (Matt. 16:24–25).
- "For if we have been united with him in a death like his, we will certainly also be united with him in a resurrection like his. For we know that our old self was crucified with him so that the body ruled by sin might be done away with, that we should no longer be slaves to sin— because anyone who has died has been set free from sin" (Rom. 6:5–7).
- "I have been crucified with Christ and I no longer live, but Christ lives in me. The life I now live in the body, I live by faith in the Son of God, who loved me and gave himself for me" (Gal. 2:20).
- "And as for us, why do we endanger ourselves every hour? I face death every day—yes, just as surely as I boast about you in Christ Jesus our Lord" (1 Cor. 15:30–31).

In one passage, the pattern of death and resurrection is on stunning display as the apostle Paul explains his calling as a foundational leader in the church:

I will boast about a man like that, but I will not boast about myself, except about my weaknesses. Even if I should choose to boast, I would not be a fool, because I would be speaking the truth. But I refrain, so no one will think more of me than is warranted by what I do or say, or because of these surpassingly great revelations. Therefore, in order to keep me from becoming conceited, I was given a thorn in my flesh, a messenger of Satan, to torment me. Three times I pleaded with the Lord to take it away from me. But he said to me, "My grace is sufficient for you, for my power is made perfect in weakness." Therefore I will boast all the more gladly about my weaknesses, so that Christ's power may rest on me. That is why, for Christ's sake, I delight in weaknesses, in insults, in hardships, in persecutions, in difficulties. For when I am weak, then I am strong.

—2 Corinthians 12:5–10

"I delight in weaknesses, in insults, in hardships, in persecutions, in difficulties." What a contrast to the rhetoric we've grown so accustomed to hearing in our American Christian culture. We talk endlessly about being "world changers" who have churches that grow "exponentially." We are obsessed with triumphalist positivity. We hold conference after conference and workshop after workshop to unlock more material success. Our values are "the bigger, the better." The shinier, the better. The more media coverage, the more likes and shares, the more sold-out shows and events, the better. We are a mess of consumerist obligations, desperately seeking identity in what the church can acquire. We are drowning in the metrics of spiritual achievement.

We are still selling happiness.

Even in the realm of church planting, we have bought into these metrics, convincing ourselves that an ever-evolving set of strategies will surely lead us to the promised land of a brand new megachurch/multichurch empire. Our church plant was small, but

I still desperately wanted it to succeed, and to make a mark and "leave a legacy." And I held it so tightly, allowing myself to drift into anxiety and frustration that skewed my perspective. But even when success is achieved, consumerist obligations still lead us off the kingdom course. They are no sign of health, no measure of mission. They are first-half-of-life exercises in idealism that barely scratch the surface of who the church really is, her true self.

In the words of theologian Stanley Hauerwas, "Church growth strategies are the death gurgle of a church that has lost its way."[2]

And this apocalypse is begging us to recognize that. To get off the course of strategy and obligation and back to the pursuit of kingdom mission—or else.

Consider this:

- What if instead of consumerist programs and self-help sermons, we centered everything we do and say in the person of Jesus portrayed in the Gospels, and the vision of God's kingdom that permeates all of Scripture?
- What if instead of pursuing superficial relevance to attract more and better, we put down roots deeply into our religious tradition?
- And what if instead of perpetuating institutions by any means necessary, we sought to discern what the Spirit is already doing outside the four walls, in the neighborhood, for the sake of God's mission and God's justice?

In an empire that urges us to sell happiness to push forward, rise up, and accumulate more, what if we embraced the counter-intuitive way of finding our center, going deep, and facing out?

For when we are weak, humble, repentant, real, then we are strong.*

In the words of author Rachel Held Evans, "[L]ately I've been wondering if a little death and resurrection might be just what the church needs right now, if maybe all this talk of waning numbers and shrinking influence means our empire-building days are over, and if maybe that's a good thing. Death is something empires worry about, not something gardeners worry about. It's certainly not something resurrection people worry about."[3]

Amen.

•   •   •

Father Richard Rohr talks about the difference between the true self and the false self. The false self is bound up in our outward identity—title, achievement, success, image. But our true self goes back much farther; it is who we really are, who God has made us to be, our bedrock of belovedness, which cannot be changed or taken away. The false self, Rohr says, "will and must die in exact correlation to how much you want the Real."[4]

In one of my final sermons to our dwindling church plant, I talked a little bit about grace:

Grace is surrender.

Grace, really, is giving up.

It's giving up on self, and it's giving up on striving. It's giving up plans and dreams and hopes. It's giving up your vision. It's giving up on the purpose and direction that you

---

* 2 Corinthians 12:10.

hold dear and precious, like Paul did when he experienced insults and hardships and persecutions that rudely inter-rupted his purpose and direction.

Grace is that kind of giving up.

Grace is often the death of what is most dear.

Sometimes, grace is the death of your life's work. The death of the thing that you have poured every waking moment into, for years. The thing that has caused you to stay awake for countless sleepless nights. The thing that you dedicated every ounce of who you are to build, every drop of blood in your heart expended until you have nothing left. Grace is watching that work fall apart, assailed and attacked until it comes crumbling down bit by bit, stone by stone.

Grace is the very soft place of defeat and death.

Our church had to die for deeper health to come to everyone involved, including myself and my little family. And while it took some darkness and deconstruction for my heart to accept the words I shared that day, I finally did, and I felt free.

Because with that death came the death of my false self, of the outward attachments that had become entangled with my core identity. The calling that was my desperate obligation, but was not, despite what I had long believed, who I really was. As I experienced that death in my life, painful as it was, and as I learned to let go little by little, I began to experience more peace, more freedom, more clarity, more direction. I began to finally see and know my true self, to embrace the real underneath the shoulds and oughts. And finally, to experience the sense that my family and I were truly graduating.

Graduating from a perspective on ourselves, on God, on life, on church, everything. Graduating from a religious way of operating that is rooted in obligation rather than in the true self and the deeper life. Graduating from a system of values and measures that are stuck in the egocentrism of the first half of life.

And not a moment too soon. Rob Bell, the author who famously left the pastorate at his midwestern megachurch for a less institutional path, once said, "If the sitcom is funny for five seasons, they make seven. Most people stay too long. And what should be a graduation becomes a divorce."[5] While I never fully stopped going to church or serving the church in those few years after the closure, deep down, I was done. My wife was done. Our family was done. And once I accepted that doneness, new perspectives burst wide open. And what had been a dark and churning cynicism, still wrestling with the eruption I'd experienced, at last settled into a calming realism, an acceptance of all that had happened, an openness to all that may lie ahead.

For just as the wilderness was temporary for the Israelites, who, liberated, yet found themselves wandering and waiting for what's next, so the wilderness that you and I may have to traverse, for however long, is temporary. This deconstruction is not demolition. Not if we exit through the wilderness and to the place of promise.

Part 3

Illumination
and
Resurrection

Chapter 9

Songs of the Resurrected and the Undead

In the depths of my deconstructive season, I discovered tradition. I was done, truly done. But I felt compelled to stay connected to a church, even if I had no idea where it was all going to end up. I was homeless again, not knowing whether I would ever belong. All I knew was that I was looking for something different. And I think that that, along with the fact that our church plant had recently gathered in a downtown Methodist church, led me in a different direction than I'd ever been before.

The Methodist tradition immediately (and surprisingly) connected to something deep in my soul. It was refreshingly different. As in any good romantic comedy, it seemed I had left my hometown charismatic theology to chase the bad boy John Calvin, only to discover that it was messy-middle, liturgical-and-missional, personal-and-social-gospel John Wesley I was looking for all along.

Methodism introduced me to liturgy and mystery and history and holy conferencing and lots of committees and people who value a smart but simple faith (as well as an orderly decision-making process). Most important, Methodism, particularly this historic downtown Methodist church in Burlington, Vermont, embraced and accepted me in my darkest moment, when everything was falling apart, when I was at my most wounded. It was a time in my life when it seemed like my evangelical tribe had hung me out to dry. I attended, served, and eventually joined this church because it offered me room that I had never experienced before—room to be who I was, but also room to figure out who I was. Room to grow.

Likely that's because the church leaned more progressive, as New England Methodist churches tend to do. That is not to say there wasn't a spectrum of belief and opinion among us—there most certainly was—but a person in a deconstructive season was more than welcome. And not just welcome in a superficial sense, like the "all are welcome, but we hope to squeeze you into our mold soon enough" vibe that I'd experienced in churches many times before, but in an authentic sense. I was embraced, even as I sojourned through the desert of the real. I was somehow made to feel at home even in my spiritual homelessness.

And I was invited to serve in several capacities, helping to plan Sunday worship and even preaching a few sermons. On one particularly memorable Sunday, I not only preached the sermon but sang an acoustic anthem afterward.

The anthem I sang wasn't like the worship songs I was accustomed to singing in church. It wasn't even a Christian song. It was a popular indie-rock song about losing faith. One verse mocked the story of Adam and Eve and the fall as almost unbelievable, especially in explaining the world's everyday brokenness. Another verse brashly called out the church's hypocrisy.

I chose to sing it because it illustrated some aspect of my

sermon, but also because it captured the essence of the decon-struction happening in my life. The folks in the pews probably thought it was just clever or a relevant way of ending my talk, but for me, singing it gave me permission to consider the possibility of walking away from the church completely, to dismantle my perspective to see what I was really left with, to consider what might come next, if anything.

•   •   •

American Christian culture is fond of catchphrases and cliches. Which is not a terrible thing, but it can lead to ideas and practices that really don't have much precedent in text or tradition. A catchphrase that was hugely popular when I was growing up is "Christianity is not a religion, it's a relationship." It rose to the level of gospel truth for us, which is to say it became a soothing ideology. Maybe it is for you too.

In the '80s there was even a Christian punk-rock song that I still kind of love that bashed religion in favor of a relationship with Jesus. I remember listening to the cassette tape in our mini-van as a kid, shouting "Oh yeah!" along with the Clash-esque lead singer at the end of each religion-dissing chorus.

This straightforward idea was ingrained in me from a young age: Christianity is a relationship, not a religion, not a belief, not going to church. And an entire generation of American Christians has come to view the rituals and practices of religion as superflu-ous. This relationship, something that occurs in one's heart, rather than through external or social actions, is of supreme importance.

As with any ideology or illusion, some confusion about this relationship comes into play: Who is Jesus? What does this relationship entail? Are there any expectations? Is it just a good feeling? But at least there is a push for something more for our spiritual and emotional lives than just our outward routines.

By Ritual Alone?

During my committed New Calvinist phase, I became aware of what likely gave rise to the religion versus relationship dichotomy. The Protestant Reformers sometimes used the word religion to mean the rituals of the Roman Catholic Church that, in their minds, had become empty and hypocritical exercises in "works righteousness." The Mass, indulgences, penances, and other religious acts were showy attempts at earning merit in God's sight (while often masking secret sins and compromises), and these were an affront to a holy God who will save sinners only on the basis of Christ's merit. The doctrine of justification by faith *alone* was the antidote to all this works-righteousness religion. Trusting in Jesus with a true heart was all that should be required for right standing with God.

The massive influence of New Calvinism and the Gospel-Centered movement (a revival of Reformed theology within evangelicalism) in recent years has, at least to an extent, revived this pejorative definition of religion. There have been countless articles, plenty of books, and even a few viral videos expounding on the theme. Whether it's a set of religious works in contrast with the doctrine of justification by faith alone, or religious obligation contrasted with a heartfelt relationship with God, there is an important principle underneath all of the confusion.

Ritual alone—without an authentic and active spiritual life—is not enough.

When John Wesley contemplated the future of the Methodist movement he had founded, he expressed the same sentiment: "I am not afraid that the people called Methodists should ever cease to exist either in Europe or America. But I am afraid lest they should exist only as a dead sect, having *the form of religion without the power*. And this undoubtedly will be the case unless they hold fast both the doctrine, spirit, and discipline with which they first set out" (emphasis mine).[1]

That's some strong stuff. But Wesley doesn't fall prey to the dichotomy in those other formulations. Instead, he argues for the power of *good* religion, a power which fills its form with substance by holding fast to doctrine, spirit, *and* discipline.

Perhaps a little bit of good old-fashioned word study is in order here. Wesley is quoting 2 Timothy 3:5 when he says "form of religion without the power." Some translations like the RSV still have "religion" in this verse, while most translations have "godliness" instead. Likewise, in 1 Timothy 3:16, the NRSV has Paul saying "the mystery of our religion is great," whereas the NIV has "godliness" again. In both cases I prefer "religion" as the translation, but especially in the latter case, since this statement leads directly into reciting an early church creed or prayer. But it would seem that, in this context at least, and definitely in Wesley's usage, religion is just a formal word for the practice of godliness or piety. This can either have substance or be just an exercise in appearances. But the religion remains.

Other occurrences of *religion* in the New Testament are even more clear. In Acts 26:5, Paul talks about his former Pharisaic faith: "They have known me for a long time and can testify, if they are willing, that I conformed to the strictest sect of our religion, living as a Pharisee." And earlier, in Acts 25:19, we see a statement of comparative religion: "Instead, they had some points of dispute with him about their own religion and about a dead man named Jesus who Paul claimed was alive." In both cases, the meaning of *religion* is simply the beliefs, rituals, and practices associated with worshiping and serving God. Again, it can be one religion or another religion, good religion or bad religion, religion with substance or religion that's just an empty show. But the religion remains.

Which leads us to perhaps the most significant New Testament occurrence of *religion* in James 1:26–27: "Those who consider themselves religious and yet do not keep a tight rein on their tongues deceive themselves, and their religion is worthless. Religion that God our Father accepts as pure and faultless is this: to look after orphans and widows in their distress and to keep oneself from being polluted by the world."

James is arguing that if we assume that religion is in and of itself good, or by itself makes one good, we make a dreadful mistake. In verse 26, he takes a shot at gossips, slanderers, and accusers by reminding them all that if they can't keep a lid on it, their religion (ritual worship of God) is worthless.

One is reminded of the Old Testament prophets who harangued the Israelite religion in light of the Israelites' hypocritical injustices.[*]

And verse 27 makes the definition even clearer. Religion that is *pure* before God, James says, is to care for widows and orphans and to keep oneself from being polluted by the world. The ritual worship of God that is truly legit is the kind that, by reflex, results in caring for victims of injustice and oppression, and steering clear of systems that oppress. That's about as anti-empire as it gets.

---

[*] Amos 5:21ff.

But here's where it gets even more interesting. This bit on pure religion leads directly into James' famous diatribe on the nature of faith, works, and justification. This is where, much to the dismay of Martin Luther and his Reformation salvation scheme, James concludes, "You see that a person is considered righteous by what they do and not by faith alone. In the same way, was not even Rahab the prostitute considered righteous for what she did when she gave lodging to the spies and sent them off in a different direction? As the body without the spirit is dead, so faith without deeds is dead."

It would seem that James, in the Jewish prophetic tradition, is offering his own definition of pure, legit religion (and of true, justifying faith). It's the kind of religion that must expand beyond the ritual of worship into the good works of loving neighbors and resisting the unjust and oppressive ways of empire.

But again, religion remains. The ritual worship of God and the works it entails stand. If anything, those works are only expanded in James' exhortation, not diminished. If anything, the picture being painted is of an *integrated* religion, one that begins with sincere, heartfelt belief, continues in the heartfelt rituals of worship, and overflows into heartfelt works of service and justice in the world.

Or, as Wesley urged us to do, holding fast to the doctrine, spirit, and discipline with which we first set out. That's not ritual alone but the elements of a truly *powerful* religion.

Zombie Religion

In conversations about the decline of Christian faith in the US, a phrase is often invoked to describe the nones, dones, and millennials who aren't coming to church. They are "spiritual but not religious." Many people would use that phrase to describe themselves too. It's a straightforward way to assure someone that while you don't see the point of formal religious affiliation or practice, you are still interested, however generally, in spiritual things. Perhaps you are one of the folks who identify with that description or at least have used it to get through an awkward religious conversation.

And believe me, I get it. In the thick of my doneness, even though I was attending a church and discovering tradition, I didn't know where I was going to end up. Could I really keep doing this church thing? After everything that had happened, could I really keep it up? So much had been revealed—about the church at large, about my background, about my heart and the illusions I had been clinging to. Maybe I was going to end up being spiritual but not religious too, and simply join in the apocalyptic trend.

I think the spiritual but not religious tagline has an interesting connection to another TV show storyline. (Can you tell I like TV?) As of the writing of this book, AMC's *The Walking Dead* is the number one show on television. Where the shows I've mentioned— *Breaking Bad* and *Mad Men*—are flagships in the new-golden-age obsession with antihero dramas, *The Walking Dead* is something else entirely. It's an adaptation of a comic book focused more on the visual thrills of the zombie apocalypse genre than on the finer points of plot and dialogue. That's not to say that the plot and dialogue are weak; it's just to say that, in true comic book style, it is the graphic nature of the story that speaks volumes.

And with the detailed makeup and costuming employed to bring the zombies (called "walkers" in the show) to life, and the visual effects employed to create epically impossible survival scenarios for the main characters, *The Walking Dead* excels like no other entry in this genre before or since. But it's not all blood and guts and occasional zombie meat jackets. There is also a graphic social commentary centering on a set of survivors led by the conflicted and courageous former sheriff's deputy Rick Grimes. And when you look beneath the pile of walkers gruesomely killed by Rick and his crew, you discover the deep-seated human desire to find home, to find rest, to find flourishing, even after this apocalypse that has so devastated everything.

The show is a story about the human capacity to become just as monstrous as the walkers, just as undead and devoid of humanity and goodness. The gangs and colonies who are constantly waging merciless war on Rick and his crew demonstrate this explicitly, but Rick and his people battle the temptation to leave their humanity behind too. How do you hold on to being good in the face of your, and your species', annihilation?

When I sang that very unchurchy song in church that day, I was considering, if only to myself, the possibility of unbelief, of walking away. But that moment can't last forever, or we'll never find our exit from the wilderness and into something better. As the months wore on, I realized that skepticism and cynicism were only going to leave me empty, soulless, and detached from my humanity in Christ. They were going to leave me undead, a spiritual zombie.

The apocalypse that has visited Christian faith in America is challenging us to repent and reform *without* deconstructing ourselves to death (or undeath), without dismantling our faith to annihilation, leaving only a shell. The necessary suffering that invites us to deconstruct our empire business is not a permanent condition. It is a temporary work meant to bring us into a second-half-of-life faith, into true flourishing.

There is a way of responding to the phenomenon of the nones and dones that seems to make deconstruction a way of life. We see a growing segment of the population, the nones, demonstrating so little interest in, if not outright opposition to, the Christian faith. And we see another group that is making the careful and grievous decision to walk away from the church for good. We may think that the solution to this problem is to strip away all barriers in belief and practice to draw them back. If the cultural tide is turning in a post-Christian direction, with pluralism and secularism on the ascent, then it may seem logical to create a kind of Christianity or church that is deconstructing itself in the same direction, with no finish line in sight. This might take the shape of trying to get rid of anything rooted in the Christian text or tradition to favor a more universalizing message. It's an attempt to replace authoritative ideas about Scripture, God, Jesus, gospel, church, worship, prayer with a more universally appealing emphasis on spirituality and social activism.

Maybe it's an attempt to replace religion with relationship. Maybe it's an attempt to be "spiritual but not religious."

And to be sure, all of our ritual worship of God, and all of our practices of piety and godliness, are nothing without Spirit, nothing without activism, nothing without the power behind them. But I have come to believe that our faith will be just as empty without the rooted religious practices that give it substance, meaning, and life.

Could it be that what this apocalypse is revealing is our need not merely to be spiritual or merely to cling to religious ritual but to embrace a spiritually resurrected religion? To inhabit the rooted religious practices that can sustain us over the long haul and bring life to the world? To carry with us the spiritually transforming resurrection power of the person and presence of Jesus, even as we apply ourselves to the religious life that has shaped the church of Jesus for millennia?

Make no mistake, this apocalypse is first and foremost a great revealing of our empire business that by its nature deconstructs, sometimes devastatingly so, leading to a necessary ending. But that deconstruction is meant to preserve, not demolish; it is meant to open up a new and flourishing future, not stop at our ego death or settle in the wilderness.

It is meant to bring us home. It is meant to bring us rest in the always imperfect but beautiful space of belonging to the Spirit-filled body of Christ.

And that is no zombie religion.

·　　·　　·

There were times in my life when I sang a different song—in the thick of my controlling charismatic upbringing, or while visiting a health-and-wealth megachurch, or during my life-saving but misguided New Calvinist phase.

Or alongside our beautiful, but temporary and illusory, church plant.

They were times when I sang a song of unabashed worship.

During those times, I often found myself lost, detached from the crowd, devoid of self-consciousness, immersed in connection with Jesus. I raised my hands toward heaven without caring how it looked; I cried tears of conviction and joy and recommitment and gratitude regardless of how silly I felt. Sometimes I shouted "Yes!" for sheer joy, and other times I whispered "I'm sorry" in deep pain. And in all those times, I found the unspoken brokenness of my life, so overwhelming so much of the time, so devastating in its effects both within me and around me, repeatedly met somehow with an acceptance and assurance and a belovedness and peace that I cannot naturally explain.

When I went through my very own apocalypse and my life fell apart piece by piece, it was neither a vague spirituality nor an empty religious ritual that pulled me through. Even in the midst of such a dead and dry desert of the real, there was always one thing, and one thing only, that I held on to.

That for my whole life I have been fiercely, unstoppably drawn to Jesus.

And that when I look at him, I cannot look away.

Only he can resurrect me. Where else would I go? What other song would I sing?

· · ·

John, the Beloved Apostle, began his gospel by calling Jesus "the Light."* And that's because Jesus described himself that way: "I am the light of the world. Whoever follows me will never walk in darkness, but will have the light of life."†

The only way I was going to be resurrected from the darkness and deconstruction unleashed by my apocalypse was to come face to face with the Light of the World, the Light of life himself.

And that's the only way American Christianity will be resurrected too.

---

* John 1:4ff.
† John 8:12.

Chapter 10

Making Progress

All through my church-planting years, I was progressing. I don't mean I was becoming a card-carrying political progressive. I mean that I was discerning, in the context of the progressive city I loved, new perspectives in my theology, spirituality, and ministry.

Though this progression entailed some deconstruction, as the dust settled and the clouds cleared, it brought me to a new foundation to build on.

It brought me to the person of Jesus.

Really, it brought me back to the bedrock, to the God who had been with me all along. But I was starting to see that God in a brand-new way, as revealed in Jesus. And it changed everything.

·   ·   ·

As simplistic as it may sound, the person of Jesus revealed to us in the Gospels is the antidote to all of our empire business.

From that firm foundation, from that solid rock, we can launch into our new beginning.

My own new beginning, after my personal great revealing and necessary ending, arrived unexpectedly outside the lines in the

realness of the everyday. It arrived when the Holy Spirit inter-
rupted me in the depths of my hopeless cynicism, about two years
after the closure of our church plant, smack-dab in the middle of
the wilderness. It was right there, in that place, that God called
me out of my wandering and began the good work of healing,
restoration, and hope. My new beginning arrived in the form of
a spiritual experience not unlike John Wesley's famous "heart
strangely warmed."

And it arrived while I was watching TV. (Probably not surprising to you at this point. God speaks to me through the TV, mainly.)

The first season of HBO's *True Detective* introduced something
unique to the new golden age of TV flooded with antiheroes in spi-
rals of destruction. Detectives Marty Hart and Rust Cohle, played
by Woody Harrelson and Matthew McConaughey, certainly bear
some of the marks of antiheroes. But their stories are sadder. These
are two characters whose personal lives are torn up by trauma,
addiction, and obsession and who are suddenly thrust into a bizarre
serial-murder case with vaguely supernatural overtones.

The show hinges on McConaughey's character, a man
traumatized by the loss of his daughter, now an angry, nihilistic
atheist interested only in the evidence and rejecting all the super-
stition surrounding it. But his character undergoes a powerful
transformation in the final episode. While some have said *True
Detective* is "a ghost story with no supernatural elements,"[1] it is
Rust—not the murderous antagonist—who introduces something
profoundly spiritual.

After the climactic confrontation in which Rust and Marty are
nearly beaten by the killer but overtake him in the end, both end
up in the hospital. Rust awakens from a coma and tells his partner
what he saw "in the dark": "It was like I was a part of everything

that I ever loved . . . I could still feel her love there, even more than before. And there's nothing, nothing but that love."

As McConaughey's character began to sob, so did I. I could sense that his conversion was somehow exactly the conversion I needed, that as this character's despair was so suddenly overwhelmed by love, mine was too.

Marty directs Rust's attention to the star-filled night sky and asks him to make up a story, like he used to when he was a kid. Rust replies, "There's only one story, the oldest. Light versus dark."

This finale episode is titled "Form and Void," and the allusion to Genesis 1 is clear. It was there, in the earliest moments of history, that the light first battled the dark. The earth was formless and void and so very dark. And God said, "Let there be light."

Marty's response to Rust is well intentioned—when you look at the night sky, it sure seems like the dark has a lot more territory than the light. But moments later Rust corrects him, and a season-long narrative reaches its crescendo: "You're looking at it wrong, the sky thing. Once there was only dark. You ask me, the light's winning."[2]

In a blog post the next day, I wrote,

The previous cynical and nihilistic personality of the character makes these words astounding—impossible, even. But there he was, on the screen, confessing an entirely new perspective on the world and his own life. And there I was, in my IKEA recliner, beginning to experience something very similar . . .

There were ugly tears and guttural prayers and unexpected words coming out of me from I don't know where. There was conviction—but not in the dramatic shameful sense, in the sense of confident belief moving into the place where there has long been pain and questioning and confusion. There was that strange sense of coming home, of fog clearing, of a hope and a future emerging, materializing, as if out of nowhere . . .

As for me, I am going forward, and I'm not going back, because I believe—I mean, I really believe—that the light is winning.

I experienced a kind of resurrection that night. I sensed the strange and sudden movement of the Spirit stirring the dark waters of my soul, propelling me into the second half of life, opening up something far better and more spacious than anything I'd ever known. What I didn't know then is that this new beginning would envelop me in a new process of reclaiming the true, the good, and the beautiful amid all of the pain and heartache in my life, an acceptance of all that had been revealed, and all that had come to an end, alongside an embrace of all that I could carry with me into the future. It was the start of coming full circle, in a whole new way.

And it was all of those things because I had finally come face to face with the Light. It was Jesus who met me that night, Jesus who changed me, Jesus—the Light!—who resurrected me. The apostle Paul's words are perfect here: "For God, who said, 'Let light shine out of darkness,' made his light shine in our hearts to give us the light of the knowledge of God's glory displayed in the face of Christ."*

Where else would we go? Everything changes when we begin to believe the light is winning.

* 2 Corinthians 4:6.

God, Revealed

If you've been involved in the conversation around the cultural shift taking place since the turn of the millennium, and what it means for the church, you've probably heard of David Kinnaman and Gabe Lyons' book *UnChristian*. That book is based on their research with the Barna Group on how the rising generation of American millennials views the Christian faith. Their findings became definitive for my generation of leaders and sparked a wave of new churches and initiatives. One of those churches was our church.

Among the most influential of Kinnaman and Lyons' observations is that the vast majority of millennials view American Christianity as too judgmental. And the culture's perspective implies a corrective for the church: "They say Christians are more focused on condemning people than helping them become more like Jesus."[3]

A couple of years later, Lyons built on this research in an attempt to describe what the next Christians might look like. He offered this sobering observation in the process: "To many onlookers, Christianity has become a parody of itself."[4]

After a number of books and projects that continued building on this research, Kinnaman and Lyons teamed up again in 2016 to publish a new book, called *Good Faith*, based on updated research. In this book, there is an interesting shift in their approach to the data, a shift from critiquing American Christianity to preserving and advancing orthodoxy in the face of cultural opposition. The culture's labeling of Christianity as "irrelevant and extreme"[5] is now more misguided than it is helpful. Hence, "This isn't just a feeling. When one third of college-aged adults want nothing to do with religion, and 59 percent of Christian young adults drop out of church at some point in their twenties, it's the new reality on the ground. Culturally, it seems like a landslide victory for the other side . . . whoever that is."[6]

And:

- "More than two out of five Americans believe that, when it comes to what happens in the country today, 'people of faith' (42 percent) and 'religion' (46 percent) are part of the problem, rejecting the idea that religious individuals could be part of the solution.
- "More than eight out of ten practicing Christians say religious freedom has become more restricted because some groups are actively trying to move society away from traditional Christian values.
- "Today only one-fifth of US adults strongly believe that clergy are a credible source of wisdom and insight when it comes to the most important issues of our day."[7]

And so the authors' project has moved from deconstructing the status quo to rebuilding and defending our good faith. In a broad sense, Kinnaman and Lyons are mapping out what a new beginning might look like after the apocalypse of decline and the shift to a post-Christian culture. And the way they describe the good faith that we so desperately need in this new beginning is really quite beautiful:

The secret recipe for good faith boils down to this: how well you love, what you believe, and how you live. If you don't have all three, your faith isn't good—it's half-baked . . .[8]

When we relate to people who are not Christians, whether secular or another faith, we have to get the love + believe + live = good faith equation right. As our friend Barry Corey says, Christians should have "soft edges and firm centers." Jesus related to people this way . . .

When we have soft edges and firm centers, we can see people Jesus dearly loves. And when, aided by the Holy Spirit, we see them, we can look beyond the trends and into real people's hurts, hopes, and needs.[9]

This is a vision for the kind of faith that doesn't become zombified by losing the essential firm center of belief or by neglecting the embodied practices of loving and living well. It's a vision we desperately need, especially with the threat of deconstructing ourselves to death. Good faith is resurrected faith, the kind that can't be held down by the shifting and transition that have come to us in these apocalyptic times.

But there is something I want to add to Kinnaman and Lyons' proposal—or maybe a caveat I want to propose: we run the risk, in taking on the posture of preserving and advancing orthodoxy, of slipping back into the status quo illusion, of dismissing all challenges to our way of doing things as nothing more than unregenerate, unsaved, nonelect, nominal nonsense, dismissing our apocalyptic moment and refusing the opportunity to repent and reform.

There's no shortcutting to the new beginning without the necessary ending.

And that new beginning pivots not just on a sense of orthodoxy but on how we understand and relate to Jesus himself.

* * *

I want to extend an evangelistic sort of invitation to you. You don't have to respond to it, at least not right away. You can take all the time you need to mull it over. You don't have to bow your head, close your eyes, or walk down an aisle. But this really is a "come to Jesus" moment, because I want to invite you, right now, to consider the life-changing importance of becoming Jesus-centered.

I don't think our faith—your faith or my faith or the Christian faith in America—is going to survive unless it becomes firmly centered on him.

If we're going to keep doing this Christianity thing and invite others to do it with us, then how we see and understand God will make all the difference. As lifesaving as my stringent New Calvinist worldview once was to me when I was drowning in inconsistencies, its vision of God just couldn't sustain me. And when it was compromised even more by right-wing political agendas and culture-war tactics, it became even more harmful. The result was a God who wanted war, a vengeful, wrathful, punishing God we needed to *avoid* by trusting in the sacrifice of Christ. This was a God who made me want war too, who turned me into an antagonistic debater of the people around me rather than a compassionate and empathetic friend. This was a God who called me to take up arms in the culture war rather than engage that culture for the sake of the good news of peace.

This was a God whose controlling character, picking and choosing who he will save and who he will damn just to display his power, became the basis for a controlling church leadership that used the threat of damnation to keep people in line. This was a God who gave men special authority, enabling male leaders to demean women and refuse their wisdom and leadership. This was a God whose unhinged anger toward sin justified the exclusion of so many on the basis of cultural differences and identities that fell outside of institutional lines. This was a God whose message of salvation was primarily for individuals wanting to be justified by faith alone in order to escape hell, not something facing outward for the sake of God's mission and God's justice in the world.

Thankfully, the beloved apostle John gives us a strong push in a much better direction, toward a more beautiful vision of God, a vision that can sustain us through these apocalyptic times and lead us into a flourishing faith, our new beginning.

We've seen that John calls Jesus "the Light," but here's where he's really going with that:

> In the beginning was the Word, and the Word was with God, and the Word was God. He was with God in the beginning. Through him all things were made; without him nothing was made that has been made. In him was life, and that life was the light of all mankind. *The light shines in the darkness, and the darkness has not overcome it . . .*
>
> The Word became flesh and made his dwelling among us. We have seen his glory, the glory of the one and only Son, who came from the Father, full of grace and truth . . .
>
> *No one has ever seen God, but the one and only Son, who is himself God and is in closest relationship with the Father, has made him known.**

Jesus is the light because he illuminates and reveals who God really is. John goes so far as to say that no one had ever seen God

---

* John 1:1ff., emphases mine.

the Father, really seen him, until Jesus made him known to us. This is an incredible statement that humanity was largely dealing in types, shadows, metaphors, impressions until the Word, the Logic of God, the one and only Son, became a fleshy human being and fully revealed God's character and nature to us!

The apostle Paul adds that "the Son is the image of the invisible God,"* our only way of seeing and knowing who God is. Part of this great revealing is an opportunity to finally see God as God really is, by seeing who Jesus really is. And that's an opportunity we've got to embrace if we want to press through to flourishing in this brilliant new beginning. That's a vision of light that cannot lose, that the darkness can never overcome.

We're Never Gonna Survive Unless...

Back when I was a New Calvinist, there was a lot of talk about a christological hermeneutic—or, in layperson's terms, a Christ-centered interpretation of the Bible. The big idea was that we needed to "see Christ in all of Scripture," including the Old Testament, in order to get the Bible right. And this seemed really good and even exciting for a while as we all tried to rethink our understanding of Old Testament stories and characters.

And so we pored over every scenario in the Hebrew Scriptures for evidences of a Christ-centered theme. And that posed a bit of a problem when we hit some of the bloodier, more violent, and downright disturbing stuff—like that time when the sons of Jacob slaughtered a bunch of dudes who were recovering from spur of the

---

* Colossians 1:15.

moment circumcision.[*] The senior pastor of our Calvinist Baptist church preached a sermon on that, focusing on the fact that the sons of Jacob, of Israel, the "seed of the woman," had plundered the heathens (you know, after murdering them while they were still in pain). And this plundering is redemptive, foreshadowing Christ.

Because, you see, Christ is all about redemption.

It wasn't just a weak connection, a total stretch; it was also deeply flawed. In this version of being Christ-centered, "Christ" is really just code for the Reformation doctrine of penal substitutionary atonement (or PSA for short). What we were really looking for in the Old Testament was not a glimpse or precedent or unfolding narrative of the person of Jesus so much as stories that fit the pattern of a highly Reformed and Calvinist vision of the atonement. For New Calvinists like us, that was really all there was to understand about Jesus. He's the one who dies. And in so doing, he's the one who satisfies the bloodthirsty wrath of God that we all deserve, by letting God torture him on the cross in our place. And yes, he's the one who rises, but that's just an afterthought to his real purpose for existing, which is to redeem the elect (the "seed of the woman") from hell.

I had a conversation with that senior pastor just as Kalen and I were in the early stages of planting our church. He was curious about what I was going to preach in our early services. I had planned on preaching through the Gospel of Luke.

He pressed me, asking which commentaries I would be using. I don't think my answer was up to his New Calvinist standards, because he gave me a hushed and deep-toned warning: "Be careful preaching the Gospels. They scare me to death."

---

* Genesis 34:24ff.

And it hit me—the Christ-centeredness preached so ada-
mantly by this pastor was not really Christ-centered at all.

Or to be more particular, it was not Jesus-centered.

●   ●   ●

While that pastor and his church were proudly part of the rising
Gospel-Centered movement, they were really not gospel-centered
at all.

Or more particularly, they were not *Gospels*-centered.

This is why I am convinced that the church will not be
able to survive the challenges of this century unless we get a lot
more Jesus-centered. Being Jesus-centered is a way of seeing God,
Scripture, and all of life as deeply rooted in the person of Jesus
as portrayed in the Gospels. This does not negate any other part
of Scripture, particularly the rest of the New Testament, but it
provides both an interpretive lens and an anchor point for our
understanding of the rest. Jesus becomes the Light who illuminates our interpretation of Scripture itself. The Word made flesh
becomes the standard by which to measure the words on the page.

With God the Father, we acknowledge (along with John,
the Beloved Disciple and Revelator) that only Jesus has revealed
him to us. God is like Jesus—during the second advent (seen at
the end of John's Apocalypse) just as much as the first (seen in
John's Gospel). Really! Truly! This great revealing is about seeing
who Jesus really is. As pastor Brian Zahnd summarizes in a mini
modern-day creed, "God is like Jesus. God has always been like
Jesus. There was never a time when God was not like Jesus. We
haven't always known this, but now we do."

If God is like Jesus, can God be the bloodthirsty, hellbent, wrath-venting redeemer depicted in the Calvinist "Christ-centered" vision? May it never be! Jesus shows us a God whose love for friends and enemies overcomes all, who sacrificially settles our debt to sin with the poured-out love gift of himself. And who rises from death to give us the greatest gift of all—life abundant and eternal when sin and Satan (who exists to steal, kill, and destroy, while Jesus came to give life)* demand death.

With Scripture, we center the whole narrative, all sixty-six books, on the person of Jesus portrayed in the Gospels. This does not make any other part of the Bible less true but defines its truth based on how it connects to and reflects on the truth embodied by Jesus. Jesus is the Word of God (becoming flesh and blood!), and the Bible testifies to him. As New Testament scholar N. T. Wright has often said, this means we read Paul in light of Jesus and the Gospels, not the reverse. And the Old Testament is authoritative too, insofar as the Spirit inspired its narrative witness to the person of Jesus (not as an inerrant textbook for various historical and theological facts).

If Scripture is centered on Jesus, can we really "see Christ" in the murdering and plundering of Jacob's primitive and violent family? May it never be! Jesus never lifts the sword and chooses the way of peace when confronted by his empire enemies, even to the point of death. God was not redeeming the elect ones through bloodshed but redeeming the whole world despite it, giving narrative glimpses and Spirit-spoken whispers and progressively unfolding hints of his full revelation in the person and work of Jesus, whom the prophets called the "Prince of Peace." (Those glimpses and hints are what we should be looking for

---

* John 10:10.

in the Old Testament, rather than imposing some Reformation-derived formula.)

Finally, in all of life, we seek to make the person of Jesus the main thing, shaping our views of self, others, and the world with the mold that he gives us in the Gospels. This doesn't mean we become passive hippies seeking to avoid the world's pain, because Jesus didn't do that. Jesus confronted it all head-on, calling spades spades, and swords swords. His was a courageous peace, one that stood against the evil of the empire and the abuses of the religious establishment on behalf of all the oppressed and marginalized. Yet it was also a peace that would not participate in the violent political "othering" of Romans and Samaritans, or Rome's "othering" of everyone else. His was a kingdom of justice and peace that superseded the violent empires of men. And the violent empire, along with the violent religious establishment, executed him for it.

If all of life is centered on Jesus, can we really justify any other way, as those who claim to follow him, who bear the name Christian, or who want to be centered on his gospel? May it never be!

And may it never be that we promote or tolerate those other ways, powerful though they may seem, as supposed Christians seeking political power advocate horrendous policies such as gun proliferation, racist deportation, assaultive misogyny, and unending war, because these ways are all passing away.

When asked how he would wish to pass on his faith to the next generation, N. T. Wright summed up this Jesus-centeredness better than I ever could:

I think I want to tell them, just read the Gospels more. Many Christians in our day treat the Gospels, as a friend of mine said, as the optional chips and dips at the beginning of the meal, which, you could just take it or leave it, there's some nice stuff to crunch there. But then you go and sit at the table and have the red meat of Pauline theology, and that's where we're all, as it were, headed. And I want to say, look, I love Paul, Paul is fantastic, he's been the stuff of my life. But, the dynamism of the Gospels and the person who walks out of those pages to meet us, is just central and irreplaceable . . .

Jesus is absolutely in the middle. If you want to know who God is, look at Jesus. If you want to know what it means to be human, look at Jesus. If you want to know what love is, look at Jesus. If you want to know what grief is, look at Jesus. And go on looking, until you are not just a spectator but you're actually part of the drama which has him as its central character.[10]

This, and nothing less, is the essence of good faith.

＊　　＊　　＊

When it comes right down to it, there is only one antidote to our empire business. And that is Jesus.

That's why that woman with the alabaster jar anointed the one true king for his burial—because in a world where we always have the empire with us, only Jesus can inaugurate and consummate a new kind of kingdom.

Jesus, and not Caesar or any American politician, is Lord. Jesus, and not any church leader with a controlling, authoritarian agenda, is Lord. Jesus, and not any institution bent on excluding others to insure its own survival, is Lord. Jesus, and not military might or consumerist achievement, is Lord. All the false gods of sinful human empire are, and shall be, brought low in the Messiah, in the liberating King, in Jesus.*

And it bears saying this too: Jesus, and none of our idealistic ego dreams of being relevant and popular and successful, or solving all the church's problems and making our mark, is Lord.

In the shadow of empire, Jesus is calling his people to follow him into another way, a way marked by humility, simplicity, justice, and peace. As many segments of the church scramble for new programs and ideas and accessories to draw more people in, Jesus is calling us out again. As so many search for ways to be more relevant and pursue American metrics of spiritual achievement, Jesus is calling us to find our center, go deep, and face out.

This is what will sustain us for the generational long haul, through this apocalyptic transition and after. Not more programs and obligations, but simply looking at Jesus, and not looking away.

---

* Luke 1:51–53.

Chapter 11

Resurrected Religion

The rallying cry of "spiritual but not religious" in this apocalyptic moment is well intentioned, and it might even be helpful as some of us process the eruptions taking place in our faith and life. But like a vision of God that isn't centered on Jesus, it will not sustain us. Nor will it renew, reform, or sustain the Christian faith in America.

The goal is to arrive not at a status quo faith or some semblance of faith or a vague version of faith but at a flourishing faith. To step into our brilliant new beginning, both personally and collectively, we need to first find our center in the person of Jesus.

And then we need to go deep.

●   ●   ●

After having that experience with Jesus while watching the season-one finale of *True Detective*, I was lifted out of the miry cynicism into which I had sunk. The clouds of deconstruction cleared to make room for something else: hope. I wasn't out of the wilderness yet. But from the depths of my heart, I began to believe the light is winning.

Over the next months, and really the last couple of years, I found myself letting go of the things that had bound me in the dark. Slowly but surely, I was both coming to terms with the real hurt and pain of my authoritarian upbringing and my failed ministry, owning up to my season of empire business, and releasing bitterness toward those who had wronged me. I was also learning to accept myself for who I truly am despite all the contrary messages I had internalized—to finally believe that I am inherently valuable and truly enough, and to walk in my unconditional belovedness before God.

And in the midst of this new process, I was starting to sense something else: belonging.

Belonging—this is the essence of a flourishing life. To believe, as my friend Justin Carver puts it, that "I really have a place in this world." And to live, as Yale theologian Miroslav Volf puts it, "into our human and personal fullness."[1]

Volf has written the book on flourishing (titled, appropriately, *Flourishing*), in which he further defines it this way: "*Flourishing* . . . stands for the life that is lived well, the life that goes well, and the life that feels good—all three together, inextricably intertwined. I use the term interchangeably with 'the good life' and 'life worth living.'"[2]

Volf continues by naming the bookends of the biblical narrative—the garden of Eden in Genesis on one hand* and the city coming down out of heaven in Revelation on the other†—as the best images we have of human flourishing. While these are not achievable in the world as we know it (utopias are a lost cause), they can be the goal toward which we are always moving

---

* Genesis 1.
† Revelation 21.

as we seek flourishing in the "already," the here and now. And, for believers, they can be the firm expectation of what awaits us, truly and completely, in the "not yet," when King Jesus fully puts an end to sinful empire.

The larger point of Volf's work is instructive here too: in the age of market-driven globalization, religions are necessary now more than ever to make us people who "do not live by bread alone."[3] The visions of flourishing that Christianity and the church are communicating are desperately needed in these times. And so the doom and gloom responses to religious decline in the US, whether from those panicking at the potential losses or from those who would welcome the extinction of our faith, are simply not going to help us or the world find the good life.

No, the vision of flourishing for human beings and the world uniquely offered by the Christian faith is leading to flourishing for that faith itself. And the spiritual belonging that we, and the world, most need is found not in superficial strategies and obligations but by going deep into the roots of our religion. The home that I have found in this season, the home that I believe many are finding in these apocalyptic times, and the home that I hope you find too, is located down deep in the Christian tradition.

But here's the thing. If you're looking for a good faith that will translate into the good life, no matter what trends are unfolding in the culture or the church, you might need to become a bit of a rebel to find it. Here's what pastor Brian Zahnd has to say in his book *Water to Wine*:

In keeping with a healthy dose of rebellion, I unabashedly call myself religious. Self-identifying as a religious person may be one of the last acts of rebellion possible in our libertine era! In the secular West, the religious person may be the last rebel. So let me say it deliberately and with a hint of defiance: I'm not just spiritual, I'm religious. Anyone can be spiritual. Atheists are spiritual these days! So of course I'm spiritual—we all are!—but I am also intentionally religious. I accept the rigors and disciplines of a religious tradition. I do so because I refuse to leave my spiritual formation to the fads of amorphous "spirituality." I confess sacred creeds and observe a sacred calendar. Most of all I'm a religious person because I pray. Prayer is what religious people do.[4]

What Religious People Do

During my desert sojourn, the Methodist tradition connected me to an even greater tradition, the great tradition of the church: the church calendar, the lectionary, the liturgies, the prayers, the Eucharist. I'd dipped my toes into some of these things during our church plant, celebrating the advent season each year and, toward the end, orienting our gatherings around weekly communion. But it wasn't until I stepped out of that independent charismatic evangelical stream into one connected to a much deeper and more defined history and lineage that these rhythms and practices took on their real significance for me.

I remember being deeply impacted by these simple things that others would probably overlook. Like the way the pastor would say, "The Word of God for the people of God," after the lectionary reading, and everyone would respond, "Thanks be to God." Or the fact that there were lectionary readings at all—readings from the Old Testament, Psalms, Gospels, and New

Testament each and every Sunday that often just stood on their own, rather than as props for the sermon. (The Gospel readings especially impacted me, repeatedly reminding me of my need to be Jesus-centered.)

There was also the slow chantlike hymn that we'd often sing in which "Lamb of God who takes away the sin of the world, have mercy on us" was the only lyric. And the liturgies for baptisms and Holy Week services. And the prayers we read—prayed!—together. And the candle lighting. And the decorations that coincided not with national holidays but with holy days on the church calendar.

These things felt so tangible, like handholds on a climbing wall keeping me from falling. Even though I was still wandering, I was getting the sense that this may be the place I was heading—away, once and for all, from an expression of American Christianity that prides itself on religionless novelty and toward that which, for better or worse, is hearkening back to the past just as much as it is figuring out how to venture into the future. That the former is more prone to ego projection and a lack of reflection is obvious, and an obvious reason why I was feeling less and less able to relate to it while transitioning to the second half of life. It just seemed so empty all of a sudden.

But in the tradition, and especially in the Eucharist, I saw the first signs of something resembling a rooted spiritual home.

And when I reflect on it now, I can only ask where I would be without the Eucharist. It is here, at the Lord's table, in the bread and the cup, that Jesus' presence becomes the center of our religious practice. And it is here, all through my personal apocalypse, that I repeatedly met Christ in the quiet power of communion. If other spiritual experiences and breakthroughs are impossible to schedule or script, Jesus' invading our space without warning in the power of the Spirit, the Eucharist is an appointment with the crucified and risen King. And whether weekly or monthly (but preferably weekly!), it's an appointment that a rooted, sustainable, flourishing faith must keep.

And that, really, is the reason for religion. It sends the roots of our faith down deep. It drops anchor right to the bottom, connecting us to the history from which we've come. It provides handholds for our attention and our affection in the midst of all the distractions that are relentlessly competing for them. The routine and the ritual, the repetition and the rhythm—these are what shape us into the people of God. It is not a bland pursuit of cultural relevance that will sustain us over the long haul, nor is deconstructing ourselves into oblivion to keep pace with the culture, but the rooted practices that define who we are as religious people. If our Christian faith is going to flourish in the decades ahead, outward success won't matter at all. Deep substance will.

Just as we find our center in the person of Jesus, we go deep first by committing to the practice of the Eucharist. Over the past few years, the Eucharist has become the stabilizing force of my faith, tethering me through the darkness and deconstruction, anchoring me as the light and hope returned. It is, even in its simplicity, all-encompassing, containing everything I've learned about my identity in Christ. There's a simple prayer I pray every time I take the elements that reflects this. Just the other day I taught my oldest daughter to pray it too when we took communion at our Methodist church: "Lord Jesus, I am forever undeserving; yet you have declared me worthy; let me live up to your great love."

To be undeserving is not to be unworthy in a shame-based sense. It is to recognize my frailty and brokenness compared with the gracious gift of life in Christ. His broken body and shed blood are not offered to appease an unhinged, wrathful deity, as the stringent New Calvinists insist. No, the atoning bread and cup are, rather, a love gift from both the Father and the Son, conspiring to settle our debt to sin and death and place us in right standing as beloved covenant people. And that love, poured out for all of us equally in Christ, is what declares us worthy of such love. Who are we to disagree with God?

All of this is so that we can experience freedom, now and forever—the freedom of flourishing, the good faith that leads us to the good life. Our lives receive a grand purpose—a calling—from the gift itself, to live up to the love of God in Christ by serving him and the world in that same love. And it's rooted in the religious practice of the Eucharist.

The beautiful thing is that this rootedness does not render our religion static or unspiritual. The structure of religion creates room for progressing, for the creative and innovative work of the Spirit among us. Consider a Methodist pastor's adaptation of the Great Thanksgiving communion liturgy to speak more directly into our time and cultural context. I think you'll see how these words have power to shape our lives:

> The Lord be with you.
> **And also with you.**
> Lift up your hearts.
> **We lift them up to the Lord.**
> Let us give thanks to the Lord our God.
> **It is right to give our thanks and praise.**

It is right, and a good and joyful thing,
Always and everywhere to give thanks to you,
Lord God Almighty, creator of heaven and earth.
You created for yourself a world filled with diversity
and blessed by your breath of life.
Rainbow colors bloom in spring,
summer breezes bring garden delight,
and now as autumn comes our way
we see the work of your paintbrush upon every face and tree.
In mercy, while we still held to the chains of our winter,
of pride, self-righteousness, and historic egos,
you loved us steadfastly and delivered us as babes
to reflect the beauty and diversity of your grace,
to bring us into a community of love, hope, and peace.
And so,
with all your people on earth
in every place where two or more are gathered in your name
and all the company of heaven who have gone before us,
we praise your name and join their unending hymn:
Holy, holy, holy Lord, God of power and might,
heaven and earth are full of your glory.
Hosanna in the highest.
Blessed is the one who comes in the name of the Lord.
Hosanna in the highest.[5]

"In mercy, while we still held to the chains of our winter, of pride, self-righteousness, and historic egos, you loved us steadfastly and delivered us as babes, to reflect the beauty and diversity of your grace, to bring us into a community of love, hope, and peace." What a powerful prayer! Almost as if it traces our journey through early stage religion into the reality of finding our true selves in Christ. It's a second-half-of-life prayer, for a second-half-of-life faith.

Religion is not against reality, not at war with Spirit. It need not be, as Wesley warned, the form without the power. We might say that religion can get filled with the Holy Ghost. We can all become spiritual *and* religious. Pentecostal *and* liturgical. If I may be so bold, we can become eucharistic holy rollers! Religion is about worship, about ascribing ultimate worth to God in the face of Jesus Christ, and finding ourselves formed and transformed in the process. It is about the practices that invite heaven to meet earth. That is no dry, dead thing. To join in such a project is to take part in a resurrected religion.

So instead of insulting and rejecting religion, we desperately need to resurrect it. We need to recover the kind of religion Wesley urged us to cling to, the kind that begins with deeply held belief and trust in the person of Jesus and is grounded in a Spirit-driven change of heart. The kind that continues in the works and rituals of worship. (Wesley recommended "constant communion"[6] and took the sacrament almost daily.) The kind that reflexively overflows into works of justice and service and resisting the empire. This resurrected religion is not empty and undead but powerful in the way it binds us to the grace gift of abundant, eternal life in the Messiah that can end empire once and for all.

This kind of religion will enable us to believe, and go on believing, that the light is winning, that the darkness will never overcome it.

●   ●   ●

The Book of Common Prayer is perhaps the most widely used prayer book in the global church. It is filled with prayers, readings, and liturgies for all kinds of seasons and occasions, including daily and weekly prayers and collects. In his book *Water to Wine*, my friend Brian Zahnd builds on some of these prayers to create a morning prayer liturgy, one that he uses every day.[7]

It has increasingly become the liturgy that I rely on the most in an everyday sense. It, perhaps more than any other religious practice outside of the Eucharist, has shaped my faith in a brand new way. It's a vital part of this new season in my life, where I've found a spiritual home in traditions that go deep.

There's one portion of that liturgy that is particularly resonant, though. And, similar to the communion liturgy I shared earlier, it is an adaptation, a contextualized expansion, on an ancient practice—the Lord's Prayer. I'll close this chapter with this expanded Lord's Prayer, which you are more than welcome to pray aloud as you read:

> Our Father, Holy Father, Abba Father, in the heavens,
> Hallowed, holy, sacred be your name.
> From the rising of the sun, to the going down of the same,
> The name of the Lord is to be praised.
> Holy, holy, holy is the Lord God of hosts,
> The whole earth is full of your glory.
> Holy, holy, holy is the Lord God almighty,
> Who was and is and is to come.
> Thy kingdom come, thy will be done,
> On earth as it is in heaven.
> Thy government come, thy politics be done,
> On earth as it is in heaven.

Thy reign and rule come, thy plans and purposes be done,
On earth as it is in heaven.

May we be an anticipation of the age to come.

May we embody the reign of Christ here and now.

Give us day by day our daily bread.

Provide for the poor among us

As we seek first your kingdom and your justice.

May all we need be provided for us.

Forgive us our trespasses as we forgive those who trespass
against us.

Forgive us our sins as we forgive those who sin against us.

Forgive us our debts as we forgive our debtors.

Transform us by the Holy Spirit into a forgiving
community of forgiven sinners.

Lead us not into trouble, trial, tribulation, or temptation.

Be mindful of our frame, we are but dust,

We can take only so much.

Lead us out of the wilderness into the promised land that
flows with milk and honey.

Lead us out of the badlands into resurrection country.

Deliver us from evil and the evil one.

Save us from Satan, the accuser and adversary.

So that no weapon formed against us shall prosper.

So that every tongue that rises against us in accusation
you will condemn.

So that every fiery dart of the wicked one is extinguished
by the shield of faith.

So that as we submit to you and resist the devil, the
devil flees.

So that as we draw near to Jesus Christ lifted up,

His cross becomes for us the axis of love expressed
    in forgiveness,
That refounds the world;
And the devil, who became the false ruler of the
    fallen world,
Is driven out from among us.
For thine is the kingdom and the power and the
    glory, forever.
Amen.

Chapter 12

Post-Apocalyptic Christianity

If a new beginning is possible for Christian faith in the US, what might that faith look like? We've considered that it must first become truly Jesus-centered faith, or else we're never gonna survive. And we've seen that it must also go deep into the rooted religious tradition that revolves around the Eucharist, or else it won't sustain us into this brilliant future.

But for this Jesus-centered religion to bring us back to life, and not just become an undead, zombie faith, it must be filled with the Spirit and empowered for service. It must face *out* and be consumed with God's mission and God's justice in the world.

As I grew up with controlling Christianity, with empire leadership suffocating my true self, forcing me into submission, robbing me of opportunity, and setting me up for the eruption of the real that came all those years later, I saw, firsthand, all of the failures of the prosperity gospel that praises the inequality of the empire instead of the justice of the kingdom. But even in these broken, "Spirit-filled" spaces, something was instilled deep within me. For all of that Texas cult's abuses, for all of my father's authoritarianism, for all of the empire business of mixing Jesus and money, I realize that if it weren't for those years, I might never have known the power of God. I might never have known the life that revolves around abandoned worship and connection with Jesus.

I might never have known the baptism that requires no water, in which the Holy Spirit fills us up and ignites in us an undying passion for the kingdom of God, manifest right here and now, on earth as it is in heaven. And there is, at least, some much-needed saving grace in that.

* * *

My story has probably given you a pretty thorough view of how things can go bad in pursuing spiritual manifestations apart from religious rootedness (and emotional and spiritual health). But my personal apocalypse, along with this transition from the first to the second half of life, has restored my belief in the necessity of the Holy Spirit's work. As fed up as I have been, I cannot shake the deep-seated need to experience Jesus personally by the moving and manifesting of the Spirit. I want to be a part of a *new* charismatic expression of Christianity as the church continues through this apocalyptic transition.

My childhood is peppered with church services and events that were made to manipulate experiences with the Holy Spirit. Most of the time, I never fell for these contrived encounters because I never *felt* anything. And as a thinker, an internal processor, an introvert, I questioned all of it from a pretty young age.

There was the time, for instance, when I went with my class from the East Texas church school to see a female preacher from China who was leading an event nearby. At the event, our class lined up to be prayed for by this supposedly powerful woman, and she laid hands on each of us so that we would be "slain in the Spirit." For the uninitiated, that's when a person falls down on the ground (hopefully with someone to catch them), trancelike, under the power of God. All the kids from my class dropped like flies, but when she got to me, I felt nothing and kept standing. Undeterred, she kept praying for me, the frustration in her voice growing, until suddenly, her "laying on of hands" turned into open-palmed swatting of my forehead—hard. Though the power of God didn't slay me, I feared her hitting me would, so I fell down just to get some relief.

But there were other times, usually the less contrived and spectacular ones, when I had unmistakable experiences with the Holy Spirit's power, when I genuinely and deeply *felt* something, when the manifestation was beyond my comprehension.

One time, when I was a teenager, we had a prayer meeting at my family's house with some of my father's followers. Someone began to speak in tongues, aloud, and as they did, words suddenly came into my mind and formed a sentence that had the form and cadence of a prayer. But I didn't verbalize the prayer. I was too shy, too cautious to blurt out what seemed like alien words. I just kept my eyes closed and my mouth shut and wondered if these words were meant to be an "interpretation" of what the person across the room who had been speaking in tongues had said. In any case, I was too uncertain to get all prophetic in public.

Then, the unthinkable happened. Someone else in the room offered their prophetic interpretation of the tongues, and they vocalized the exact same phrase that had formed in my mind. I was stunned. To this day, I can't remember what the phrase was—because that really wasn't the point. The point was that in that moment, I knew Jesus was real. I knew God was with me. I knew that I was accepted, that I was beloved. And I knew, beyond a doubt, that the Holy Spirit had filled me and called me for a purpose in the world.

You may think all of that is just weird, and I totally get it! And honestly, I don't think any of these particular charismatic practices are necessary to arrive at the fundamental purpose of the Spirit's power and presence in our lives. The Spirit is with us, and in us, to assure us that we are the beloved of God. This is the identity that I was meant to discover in my childhood and even through my apocalypse, my necessary suffering—that despite all the brokenness in my life bearing its awful fruit, I am still, completely, totally beloved, and Jesus is still with me by the Spirit, and that I am still, somehow, after everything, called into his mission and for his purpose. Thanks be to God!

We see this in the Holy Spirit's activity on the pages of Scripture, right? The Spirit shows up in the form of a dove alighting on Jesus after his baptism, a visual sign of the Father's approval as a voice rings out, "This is my Son, the Beloved, with whom I am well pleased."[*] Jesus explains the coming of the Holy Spirit after his resurrection and ascension as the presence of a comforter, a helper, an advocate[†]—all aspects of his own ongoing presence—to continually be with us.

And the day of Pentecost, when the Holy Spirit was poured out on the disciples who were gathered in that upstairs room in Jerusalem, is a dramatic sign of approval, acceptance, and belovedness. Especially because (as many commentators believe)[1] the presence and power of Jesus by the Spirit was poured out

---

[*] Matthew 3:17 NRSV.
[†] John 14:15ff., various translations.

equally upon a large group of disciples in that room,* potentially spanning age, gender, and class, fulfilling the prophetic promise, "Your sons and daughters will prophesy, your young men will see visions, your old men will dream dreams. Even on my servants, both men and women, I will pour out my Spirit in those days, and they will prophesy."† And as the twelve apostles then took to the streets speaking in other tongues, it was a profound sign of acceptance, approval, and belovedness that all who heard them, regardless of race or cultural background, heard the good news about Jesus graciously preached to them in their own language, a gift of assurance in and of itself.

This identity of acceptance and belovedness is the fundamental gift of the Spirit, who "testifies with our spirit that we are God's children."‡ It is this same Spirit whose voice convinces us that "neither death nor life, neither angels nor demons, neither the present nor the future, nor any powers, neither height nor depth, nor anything else in all creation, will be able to separate us from the love of God that is in Christ Jesus our Lord."§

But the Spirit doesn't stop at this level of identity. The Pentecost Spirit pours out *charisma*—gifts and callings—that *all of us* might serve God, one another, and the world in a powerful way. The Spirit empowers us for works of service—a fundamentally outward-facing thing. That's the whole purpose of those gifts and callings in Ephesians 4, fostered and equipped by the foundational leaders in the church—the apostles, prophets, evangelists, pastors, and teachers. The whole point is so we all can bring our good faith, and this good life, to our neighborhoods and to the world.

---

* See Acts 1:12ff.; 2:1.
† Acts 2:17–18.
‡ Romans 8:16.
§ Romans 8:38–39.

Which has me wondering: What of my own gift, of my own call to ministry, the one that I received at such a young age, wore on dog tags around my neck? My apocalypse was, in part, a liberation from the burden of an ego-based ministry identity. But what could be left of my call after the apocalypse?

I've come to believe that if I am going to go on trusting in the Holy Spirit, then I can conclude only one thing: "God's gifts and his call are irrevocable."*

The darkness, deconstruction, and devastation that have brought me to the start of the second half of life have, I believe, also brought me to the promised reclaiming of an old calling. I believe the light is winning—I really do.

And the same goes for you. The same goes for all of us, no matter what devastation we have experienced in the life of faith. We are the completely and unconditionally beloved of God, sealed and assured and accepted by the poured out Pentecost Spirit.

And we are called to the work of the kingdom in the world.

Because the light is winning.

After the Apocalypse

I recently took an informal poll on my Facebook page, asking folks if they have ever felt done with church as we know it—the institution, the organization, the Sunday worship and weekday meeting routine that runs on our tithes and offerings. There was a strong response in the affirmative, and a variety of reasons why, some of them personal and painful, some of them more

---

* Romans 11:29.

theoretical and theological. Many of them revolved around issues with community and some sense that the belonging they had been looking for had fractured.

The mid-2000s were abuzz with new language in the Christian world. An influx of literature sparked by the significance of the millennial transition had many of us convinced that everything about American Christianity was changing, especially the way we do church. Or better, the way we do Christian community. *Community* was one of those new buzzwords, second only to *missional* in its impact on insider church-leadership discourse. (We also saw the rise of *missional communities*, which perhaps was the synthesis of this new vision for how to do church.)

Our church plant, emerging as it did from this mid-aughts transitional moment, made these buzzwords and the ideas they represented central to our identity and vision. This was how we were going to stem the tide of the decline and reach the people whom the older churches in our region were excluding. So I made community the centerpiece of my preaching, arguing Sunday after Sunday that individualistic salvation was not the point of the gospel, and that creating a new community with the power to reconcile and change our city and the world was the whole point. I coached and empowered people to lead smaller groups in different areas of the city as if they were small churches, incorporating all we were learning about doing church into each little expression. We considered ourselves a "community of missional communities," and we dove deeply into our relationships with each other and with those in our neighborhoods and friendship circles, determined to make Sunday worship more of an afterthought to "doing life together" (with the mission in mind) every single day. If the "new monastic" folks were all about intentional communities where diverse people lived together, we at least came close by trying to *be* together as much as possible.

And there were certainly some beautiful times and some powerful things that were accomplished as we did our best to put all of this into action. But a critical flaw emerged: as much as we wanted to do things differently and solve the problem of decline, we were still confronted with the reality that as a church, we had to have some kind of identity. Being all things to all people is, actually, impossible. Our attempt at decentralizing leadership to the smaller missional communities created numerous problems, power struggles, and conflicts, as some leaders tried to create their own community identity and impose it on the whole. I was suddenly thrown into the position of stating and clarifying the larger church identity and taking a stand for it. Likewise, our attempt at deemphasizing Sunday worship created more confusion than clarity as folks wondered why we were still putting so much effort into those gatherings.

My ministry experience before the church plant had me under no illusions about the fact that Christian community would be challenging. I strove to be as organized as possible in our approach to everything, first drafting it into our church constitution and then writing paper after paper to act as a baseline and reference point for all of these activities. But I made the massive mistake of buying into an illusion that, despite my best efforts, ignited a harmful strain of idealism and social immaturity in our young church. My desire to solve all the church's problems was a first-half-of-life desire. It was fraught with obligation. And it lacked the depth of identity and stability that comes from deep religious roots.

Really, my idealistic tendency unleashed something that German theologian Dietrich Bonhoeffer had described in the middle of the last century:

He who loves his dream of community more than the Christian community itself becomes a destroyer of the latter, even though his personal intentions may be ever so honest and earnest and sacrificial . . . Innumerable times a whole Christian community has broken down because it had sprung from a wish dream. The serious Christian, set down for the first time in a Christian community, is likely to bring with him a very definite idea of what Christian life together should be and try to realize it. But God's grace speedily shatters such dreams. Just as surely as God desires to lead us to a knowledge of genuine Christian fellowship, so surely must we be overwhelmed by a great disillusionment with others, with Christians in general, and, if we are fortunate, with ourselves.[2]

Bonhoeffer's "disillusionment" is much like Rohr's "necessary suffering"—both have to do with the process by which we are stripped of idealism and ideology. With the unraveling of our church plant, my sense of calling and my desire for belonging had shown themselves to be elements of a "wish dream" upended by brutal reality. And yet both Bonhoeffer and Rohr agree that this shattering of dreams, this process of suffering, is actually grace. If we experience it, and embrace the experience, then we are, according to Bonhoeffer, "fortunate."

I saw this process of disillusionment reflected in some of the responses to my informal Facebook poll. One woman wrote eloquently that the idea of forced community in churches just feels superfluous and unnecessary. She finds community, even Christian community, in her everyday life, and it's not forced or obligatory. It's natural and seamlessly connected to the rest of her reality. Others expressed a desire to abandon Sunday worship in favor of smaller group gatherings—something like a house church. This, they felt, would be a way to escape the trappings of authoritarianism in favor of something inclusive and authentic. One fellow summed it up this way: "The institution has done too much damage." Another was even more pointed: "I want to be part of a body, not a business."

One young man, a friend, intimated that his experience as a gay, biracial, Pentecostal Quaker leaves him feeling disenfranchised by most of the institutional church—conservative or progressive. He's simply not heard or accepted for who he is. He concluded, "I still dream of being in a house church, where tongue-talking, poetry reading, deep silence, delicious food, and political demonstrations are on the agenda, and I'm somehow confident that I'll someday have that." Another woman highlighted a similar spiritual dimension to her hopes for the future: "I'm trying to keep my eyes and ears focused so I can notice what the Spirit is birthing because whatever the future of the church will be, I think it is going to get better—less programmed and sermon-focused and 'get people in the doors so we can tell them why they are wrong'—and I want to be a part of the (hopefully) humble and repentant and uniting and welcoming adventure."

And this friend brought the unique perspective of being a woman and a pastor and also done:

> I felt done at one point in my life. Done with expectations, with over-functioning for people who wanted certain things from those of us in leadership without being willing to spend the time and energy themselves to create a community of love and service. Done with the limitations and expectations put on women. I was also done with myself, in

some ways. . . . I was convinced I had failed and would just continue to fail God and people. So much anger filled me.

[I began to heal] when I met another female pastor and shared my story and realized that serving alongside her would be a completely different experience. I wouldn't be alone in struggling to lead well and dealing with the pressures of leadership. I knew after talking to her that she understood what I had been through and would be an advocate and partner. I wasn't alone anymore . . . that made me able to trust and believe again. There were smaller moments too. Moments of preaching when I felt the burn within me that I was living into my calling. Moments when we "failed" together and reflected, learned and moved forward. The key for me was the "not alone-ness."

These experiences of feeling done with church and ministry point us to the real. And in doing that, they offer us, like all apocalyptic moments do, an opportunity for a way forward, a new beginning. That's why the disillusionment is "gracious." Stripped of the lies and inconsistencies, we can discern what a post-apocalyptic Christianity might look like. In these responses alone, I think there is a beautiful balance of emphases that comes through—a balance between reforming our religion *and* just living authentically as a spiritual person in the world. As this apocalyptic transition unfolds for the American church, both of these will be needed and each will inform the other. The restrictive way of the first-half-of-life church institution just won't do. Repentance and reformation are desperately needed. But disconnecting from all aspects of organized worship and rooted religious practice won't do either, or else we will lose the integration with what makes Christianity Christian. We will end up undead in our faith, just in a different way.

Father Rohr captures this perfectly when he describes his relationship to the church and the Franciscan order: "[T]he church is both my greatest intellectual and moral problem and my most consoling home . . . The formal church has always been a halfhearted bride for me, while the Franciscans have been considerably better. The Gospel itself is my full wedding partner. It always tells me the truth, and loves me through things till I arrive somewhere new and good and much more spacious."[3]

The formal church, the structure, the institution, the organization that gives us roots and places us in the great tradition, is continually, throughout history, in need of reformation. And we find ourselves at such a reformation moment. But as we process through our disillusionment, we can see it again as worth working for and bearing with even in its problematic state. And we have a "full wedding partner" in the gospel itself, in the person of Jesus, in the moving of the Spirit through all the realness of our lives, that we might live in fullness and maturity beyond the walls of any institution.

I would add that it is this vibrant spiritual life "outside the lines," and the realization that church can happen anywhere "as we go," that in turn provides us with the power to see reformation happen, and to find our faith—and even our calling to ministry in the organized church of Jesus—resurrected.

•   •   •

A post-apocalyptic Christianity that is fixed on full, abundant, flourishing life will look different from the status quo forms, however. It will rigorously put aside programmatic obligations in favor of a Spirit-filled mission. It will stop selling wish dreams about Christian community and instead equip and empower people for their own works of service in their own real lives, for God's mission and God's justice in the world.

This doesn't cancel out the church institution but rather renews its purpose. It exists *for* God's mission in the world. Even (especially?) old institutional structures can become greenhouses for missional experimentation, for fresh spiritual expressions. One thinks of the old structures that Rick Grimes and his crew seek to rebuild and inhabit in *The Walking Dead*. While their world is quite grim, they are seeking not only survival but newness of life and flourishing in those bombed-out cities and abandoned farms and rebuilt towns. For our post-apocalyptic situation, there's a clear application: these structures are to be inhabited and, somehow, redeemed. With a spiritual kind of religion practiced at the center, the heavenly realities of church can overflow from there, can truly happen anywhere.

And this overflow into mission is a decidedly spiritual endeavor. It is a function of the moving of the Pentecost Spirit in fresh ways outside the bounds. Perhaps we don't yet even know what this movement will produce, but now is the time to begin experimenting! Missiologist Alan Roxburgh describes this perfectly when he surveys the declining "Eurotribal" churches and denominations in the West:

> The cultivation and resourcing of interconnected, localized networks determining their own challenges, actions, and responses to the shifting changes of their environments should become the primary focus and work of denominational structures and their staffs . . .

The exciting thing about these proposals is that already, across denominational systems and among congregations, in all kinds of off-stage ways that can't be immediately measured or quantified, people in differing local contexts are becoming the incubators of a new imagination with their own tentative experiments in the local . . .

Usually, such experimenting isn't organized . . . But make no mistake, it is also precisely the way in which the Holy Spirit goes about new creation (2 Cor. 5:17).[4]

Roxburgh makes it clear that the key to all of this new missional activity is listening to God and seeing what God is already doing in the places we inhabit. It's *God's* mission *out there* that we are joining, not our programmatic or strategic plans, our attempts at getting millennials or whomever back in to bump up the numbers. Jesus is already at work to renew and restore and resurrect all things, a mission underway by the power of the Spirit, beyond the shell of undead religion. And this is what brings the good life to the church, as the church brings the good life to the world.

Or, in the succinct words of my denomination, the United Methodist Church, "We think church is more than a place to go. We think church can happen anywhere."[5]

It's time to embrace the great revealing that has come to us, along with the necessary ending to the status quo, so that we can step into this Spirit-filled new beginning that is bursting with the potential for flourishing—for us, for our faith, and for a world broken under the weight of oppressive empire.

●   ●   ●

Old Testament scholar Walter Brueggemann introduced us to the terminology of "military consumerism" to describe the way of the American empire. But when he speaks of the role of the church in light of this, his description is undeniably Spirit-centered. It is well-nigh Pentecostal: "The church is the meeting that hosts *the Words From Elsewhere,* and if we do not host the Words From Elsewhere, we have become . . . a *chaplain for the empire.* Everything depends on the Words From Elsewhere"[6] (emphases mine).

"The Words From Elsewhere"! Kind of like those words that appeared in my mind during that living-room prayer meeting, assuring me of my belovedness and God's kingdom call on my life. I'm not saying that these words need to come through an experience of speaking in tongues or receiving a supernatural interpretation. Nor am I saying that they have to take on a charismatic shape. But we desperately need the supernatural words that come from outside our empire system and bring a blast of kingdom light. This is why we need religion and even the church: because that's the only structure through which the Spirit can speak the Words From Elsewhere. Everything depends on these words because the empire you always have with you. And only Jesus, by the Spirit, through the church, can bring the peace, justice, and freedom of the kingdom of God, on earth as it is in heaven.

Post-apocalyptic Christianity is a uniquely Spirit-filled Christianity. And it's a kind of faith that goes deep into the Wesleyan tradition itself. John Wesley famously said, "The world is my parish," as he launched out into open-air preaching and taught his followers to pursue social holiness and justice. And this was because of the uniquely spiritual emphasis that Wesley had received from the mystical Moravians. In their short but excellent book, *The Holy Spirit*, Stanley Hauerwas and William Willimon note that "[charismatic] Enthusiasm (infused with God) was a frequent charge against John Wesley and the Methodists."[7]

And this is where I find myself today, in the early stages of my new beginning, after my own personal apocalypse. I am leaving behind shallow roots and unsustainable (and often harmful) practices. I want rooted religion that will sustain our faith over the generational long haul. But I have no interest in abandoning that personal and powerful work of the Spirit, who assures us of our belovedness and empowers us to walk in our gifts and calling. I want my faith and life to be animated by that "charismatic enthusiasm," yielding a seamless life of humble holiness with prophetic and even political utterance.

Because, believe it or not, Pentecost is political.

Here's Hauerwas and Willimon once more:

Through word, sacrament, and ministry the Spirit makes us witnesses to Jesus Christ . . . Such a mission is required because the disciples were to make known to the world that Jesus, not Caesar, was Lord. That claim was not an attempt by Christians to grab power and to take over the role of Caesar; they proclaimed that Jesus' lordship was more radical than Caesar ever imagined. The witness of the disciples entailed a politics that was more threatening than Rome and all other worldly powers could comprehend. It is therefore not surprising that the disciples found themselves constantly in trouble. Why was the church so disruptive and threatening to controlling politicians? Blame it on the out-of-control Holy Spirit.[8]

Pentecostal Politics

A post-apocalyptic Christianity will face outward for the sake of God's mission and God's justice in the world. The Holy Spirit is unleashed in us so that we might show the world that Jesus, and not Caesar, is Lord. This takes place when we express the kingdom in our real lives, outside the lines.

And the kingdom of God is not an ethereal, detached, apolitical concept. While the kingdom is "not *from* this world,"* our task is to work for its manifestation *in* this world as it is in heaven. And that means the church becomes a politic that impacts the politics of the world in which we live.

N. T. Wright says "the kingdom of God was itself, and remained, a thoroughly political concept," and "Jesus' death was a thoroughly political event."[9] He adds, "It is time, and long past time, to reread the gospels as what we can only call political theology—not because they are not after all about God and spirituality and new birth and holiness and all the rest, but precisely because they are."[10]

Recognizing the political nature of the kingdom of God and the Gospels does not give Christians permission to go full-steam ahead into nationalistic American politics on whichever issues they perceive as being godly or biblical. Instead, it calls for a serious investigation into the politically charged context of the first century, and the Roman Empire (and Israelite empire business as it compromised with the way of empire) always in the New Testament background. It calls for a serious (and careful) application of Jesus' words and actions to the empire politics of our time, to see in what way the politics of Jesus and his kingdom may be prophetically speaking to our own situation (as the Words From Elsewhere).

---

* John 18:36, alternate translation.

And if we are paying attention, I think we'll discover three big things about the political theology of the person of Jesus. First, that Jesus and his kingdom are relentlessly inclusive—welcoming the outsiders, be they gentiles, women, sinners, tax collectors, the poor and oppressed, or the sick and disabled. Second, that Jesus and his kingdom are economically just, turning the tables on the social strata and welcoming beggars from the highways and byways to the feast. And third, that Jesus and his kingdom are nonviolently peaceable, warning against retaliation and calling for enemy love instead. The way forward for American Christianity—our new beginning—lies in becoming part of this political reality, both already and not yet.

The one way for the American church to make sure that Jesus will have nothing to do with us in the years ahead is to continually compromise with the ways of empire, to be, biblically speaking, lukewarm. It really doesn't matter if we are numerically healthy; the Laodicean church was too. That's not the measure of God's favor and Jesus' presence in our midst. What matters is that we face out and embody again the Spirit-filled gospel of the kingdom. This is an essential result of becoming Jesus-centered.

Because the way of Jesus is the way of empire resistance. And it is undeniably political. Jesus' whole mission was framed in contrast to the empire ways of power and control, first by his mother, Mary, in her prophetic Magnificat in Luke 1, and then by him in his reading of the prophet Isaiah when he began his public ministry in Luke 4. And this was in keeping with the entire prophetic tradition before him, which announced the Words From Elsewhere to the powers that be.

First, Mary: "He has performed mighty deeds with his arm; he has scattered those who are proud in their inmost thoughts.

He has brought down rulers from their thrones but has lifted up the humble. He has filled the hungry with good things but has sent the rich away empty."*

Then, Jesus himself:

He went to Nazareth, where he had been brought up, and on the Sabbath day he went into the synagogue, as was his custom. He stood up to read, and the scroll of the prophet Isaiah was handed to him. Unrolling it, he found the place where it is written:

"The Spirit of the Lord is on me, because he has anointed me to proclaim good news to the poor. He has sent me to proclaim freedom for the prisoners and recovery of sight for the blind, to set the oppressed free, to proclaim the year of the Lord's favor."

Then he rolled up the scroll, gave it back to the attendant and sat down. The eyes of everyone in the synagogue were fastened on him. He began by saying to them, "Today this scripture is fulfilled in your hearing."†

From this starting point we can see just how political Jesus' life and ministry truly were—not to mention his death and resurrection. So let's take a look at these three features of the politics of Jesus and what we can learn about them as we combat empire politics.

1. Jesus and His Kingdom Are Relentlessly Inclusive

In earlier chapters, we saw that empire business by its nature excludes. And that's because the desire for power leads to colonizing

---

* Luke 1:51–53.
† Luke 4:16–21.

and social control. Early stage ego-religion. But in Jesus' life, we see something else entirely. We see Jesus disrupting the social and religious order at every turn, extending his messianic reach to those deemed outsiders—gentiles, women, sinners, tax collectors, the poor and oppressed, the sick and disabled.* He invited many of these people to sit with him at the table, an intensely political act in the first century, showcasing friendship and equality. New Testament scholar Joel B. Green concludes, "[M]eals served pivotal societal functions . . . One may refer in particular to the practices of Pharisees, for whom meals functioned to establish 'in-group' boundaries and embody socio-religious values pertaining to ceremonial purity. Such values were . . . shared by others, including the social elite for whom the table was an expression of kin or friendship and for whom dining served to give expression to concerns for honor and reciprocity . . . Jesus protests against dining practices that were exclusionary and motivated by concerns for one's honor."[11]

The new kingdom Jesus was inaugurating in the shadow of the Roman Empire and compromised religious establishment was a kingdom of inclusion. He lifted up the humble. He proclaimed good news to those excluded by religious empire business.

But Jesus' relentlessly inclusive mission in life may be eclipsed by his death. Because Jesus was dying to be inclusive. That was the meaning of the crucifixion.

Beyond penal substitutionary atonement theory, we find a larger context that includes Israel. The cross is the Father and Son's conspired solution to Israel's unfaithfulness. It's God's *own* act of faithfulness to rescue Israel despite her unfaithfulness. And,

---

* Cf. Luke 14:1ff.; Luke 15:1–2.

of course, Israel's unfaithfulness represents the unfaithfulness of us all, and her salvation is what we too can be grafted into by faith.*

But it's really about Israel. The prophetic hope for a pathologically unfaithful and politically oppressed nation was a Messiah who would somehow ameliorate their unfaithfulness and liberate them from the empire. And given this nation's history of worshiping God through sacrifice, it makes sense that both of these problems might be solved through a scapegoat. In this case, a person who would somehow absorb all of Israel's unfaithfulness and endure the "wages," the natural comeuppance, of their sin†— the oppression and retribution of the empire, *par excellence*, by execution on a Roman cross.

One of the key ways in which Israel had been unfaithful was in their vocation as a light to the world and in their potential to welcome the world. They persistently compromised, adopting the lukewarm ways of empire—power, greed, excess, violence, oppression—and excluded those on the margins from full religious and social acceptance. During his kingdom-inaugurating life, Jesus confronted this head-on. Just before his arrest, and likely provoking his arrest, Jesus turned over the tables in the temple, which symbolized both unrighteous economy and religious exclusion.

Thus, Jesus became the true Israel, the Light of the World, the one welcoming the outsiders, eating at the table of equality and friendship with sinners.

Jesus died for Israel's sins of exclusion, for their failure to live out their mission to become a light for all nations, for their

---

* Cf. Romans 12.
† Romans 6:23.

compromise with the exclusionary and oppressive ways of empire. And as I said, what was true of Israel's unfaithfulness is no less true of all of us. Jesus "is the atoning sacrifice for our [Israel's] sins, and not only for ours but also for the sins of the whole world."* And, "now in Christ Jesus you who once were far away have been brought near by the blood of Christ."†

But it goes even farther than that: "His purpose was to create in himself one new humanity out of the two, thus making peace, and in one body to reconcile both of them to God through the cross, by which he put to death their hostility." And, "you are no longer foreigners and strangers, but fellow citizens with God's people and also members of his household."‡ And still more: "There is neither Jew nor Gentile, neither slave nor free, nor is there male and female, for you are all one in Christ Jesus."§

Through the cross, the prophetic anticipation of Israel's forgiveness and restoration was accomplished. But also the forgiveness and restoration of everyone. And the making one of two groups formerly at odds—the religious and the unaffiliated, the insiders and outsiders, the clean and the unclean, the superior and the inferior, the accepted and the rejected, the haves and the have-nots, those at the table and those eating the crumbs. Reunited as one new humanity.

Recent religious, cultural, and political events have created a heightened atmosphere of exclusion in the US. Whoever the out-group may be in a given situation—people of color, LGBTQ people, Muslim immigrants, poor people—at both the implicit level of systemic exclusion and oppression, and the explicit level

---

* 1 John 2:2.
† Ephesians 2:13.
‡ Ephesians 2:15–16, 19.
§ Galatians 3:28.

of bigoted speech and violence, the American empire continues to do as empires do. And we, as American Christians, have been complicit.

But Jesus is dying to be inclusive. And I believe a truly post-apocalyptic Christianity in America will follow his lead in a thoroughgoing politic that rejects the exclusion of empire and practices a way of life centered on the eucharistic table of friendship and equality.

Yes, the empire we always have with us. Yes, we await the fullness of inclusion and equality in the not-yet kingdom. But that kingdom has been inaugurated! It is also *already*. And if the church speaks these Spirit-filled Words From Elsewhere again, the only question is, Will we join in?

2. Jesus and His Kingdom Are Economically Just

Luke 4 functions like something of a mission statement for Jesus as he launches his messianic ministry. He quotes Isaiah 61 and appropriates it as his own: "Today this scripture is fulfilled in your hearing." And the most remarkable aspect of this reading is that it is almost entirely economic: Jesus debuts his mission as "good news for the poor."

Walter Brueggemann, in a recent series of talks, zoomed out from his definition of our American empire as "military consumerism" to give a definition of empire itself that is simply stunning, calling it "totalism":

What . . . many scholars call empire, I want to call *totalism*. That means a totally contained socioeconomic, political, educational, cultural system, outside of which there is nothing imaginable, there is nothing thinkable, there is nothing sayable, there is nothing doable. That's where we live. That was the regime of Pharaoh, that was the regime of Nebuchadnezzar, that was the regime of the Persians, that was the regime of the Romans, that is the regime of the market ideology in which we live. We live in a totalism that has monopolized all the money, all the technology, all the imagination. The money interests control the media, the courts, increasingly the universities, and have co-opted much of the church.[12]

I believe these are prophetic words. And so were the Words From Elsewhere spoken by the prophets Isaiah and Jesus, who confronted totalism. They declared a new economy based in a different kingdom, one that operates according to the principles of the Israelite Year of Jubilee or "the year of the Lord's favor." In this new economy, the empire-building principles of unregulated amassing of wealth, lavish living, generational property theft and debt, unjust conviction and imprisonment, and environmental pillaging are overturned.

Jesus came to establish true, full, and lasting economic justice. As the king ushering in a new kind of kingdom, he came to end economic and all other forms of oppression. He came to insure that true human flourishing, "the good life," the "life worth living," would be available to all, equally. This is why empire gospels of prosperity and celebrity, along with consumerist metrics of spiritual achievement, are so contrary to the core of the gospel of the kingdom; they run on the same "market ideology," as Brueggemann says, that stacks the deck for pervasive injustice and inequality.

Later in his lecture, Brueggemann defines totalism further

as "the organization of political power and economic power that is highly concentrated in the hands of people who sit on top of the pyramid, and who really are largely indifferent to the needs or suffering of people who are much farther down the economic ladder."[13]

This pyramid system runs on the fictional ideologies of laissez-faire capitalism and trickle-down economics, which both assume that all that the poor or economically oppressed must do is pull themselves up by their bootstraps or perhaps go to work for a wealthy person and all will be well. But the gap between the wealthy and the increasingly large number of people living below the poverty line only widens. Prosperity-gospel preachers would like us to think that if we just listen to them and go to their churches and give tithes and offerings, then their prosperity will rub off on us. But this is just pyramid building, making brick-bearing slaves of the people in the pews, the antithesis of the Jubilee kingdom gospel.

We live at a time when the US is both the wealthiest nation on earth and also the most unequally wealthy nation on earth.[14] We live at a time when "22.9 percent of Americans—72.4 million people—had incomes below the federal poverty line,"[15] and those most tragically affected by this are children. We live at a time when African-American people are incarcerated at nearly six times the rate of white people,[16] and more than 80 percent of African-American men have a criminal record.[17] We live at a time when America's "original sin" of the transatlantic African slave trade and the decades of oppressive segregation thereafter have robbed generations of African-American people of their property, fortunes, and potential flourishing, revealing the need for economic reparations.[18]

It is into this political reality that Jesus' gospel of the kingdom speaks so loudly, in the words of the upside-down, anti-empire Beatitudes:

> Blessed are you who are poor, for yours is the kingdom of God.
> Blessed are you who hunger now, for you will be satisfied.
> Blessed are you who weep now, for you will laugh . . .
> But woe to you who are rich, for you have already received your comfort.
> Woe to you who are well fed now, for you will go hungry.
> Woe to you who laugh now, for you will mourn and weep.*

And Jesus is not alone in his subversive economic gospel. Our religious tradition is filled with a creational ethic that opposes the prosperity and pyramid building of empire. Journalist Elizabeth Bruenig summarizes this theme in the broader Christian tradition:

> This is a gentle formulation of a conception of creation that is expressed less forgivingly by Aquinas, and even less so by the Patristics—among them Augustine, Chrysostom, Ambrose, and so on . . . that no legal rendering of property can be just if it allows a person absolute control over resources to the point that others would perish at their whim; such an arrangement would be no more just than allowing a person a claim to the air on their property so absolute that they would be blameless for shutting your windpipe to keep you from inhaling it . . .

---

* Luke 6:20–26.

If the earth was made for human flourishing, manipulating resources to guarantee human demise is straightforwardly sinful. Simple enough.[19]

Prosperity and pyramid building are about *me*. Flourishing is about *we*.

I grew up poor, in an authoritarian home filled with financial desperation and spiritual confusion about what constitutes an honest, modest, and flourishing life. The struggle and harm inherent in that experience cannot be overstated. (Just one more reason why when I look at Jesus, I cannot look away.) And so much more so for those who possess much less privilege than I do.

Yes, the empire we always have with us. Yes, we await the fullness of economic justice in the not-yet kingdom. But that kingdom has been inaugurated. It is also already. Again, will we join in?

3. Jesus and His Kingdom Are Nonviolently Peaceable

Once upon a time, I wanted war. And I was wrong. I should have known this, should have heeded the Words From Elsewhere spoken by Jesus himself: "But to you who are listening I say: Love your enemies, do good to those who hate you, bless those who curse you, pray for those who mistreat you. If someone slaps you on one cheek, turn to them the other also. If someone takes your coat, do not withhold your shirt from them. Give to everyone who asks you, and if anyone takes what belongs to you, do not demand it back. Do to others as you would have them do to you."*

An American Christianity that so readily aligns itself with the weapons of war, that stakes its claim on the proliferation of

---

* Luke 6:27–31.

guns, that places its trust in violent retaliation is in the empire business, not the kingdom business. And we will reap the fruits thereof, just like Jesus' first-century religious community. He wept for them: "If you, even you, had only known on this day what would bring you peace—but now it is hidden from your eyes."* Conversely, "Peacemakers who sow in peace reap a harvest of righteousness."†

Yes, it's true, the empire we always have with us. Yes, we await the fullness of the nonviolent peaceable kingdom in the not-yet. But that kingdom has been inaugurated. It is also already. One last time, in this, our new beginning, after the apocalypse, after all has been revealed, will we join in?

---

* Luke 19:42.
† James 3:18.

Chapter 13

The Light Is Winning

Believing the light is winning is not turning a blind eye to brokenness. It's not working up artificial positivity. It's not denying the realities being revealed. And it's definitely not excusing and preserving the status quo at all costs.

No, believing the light is winning happens only after we embrace the apocalypse that is upon us, whether in our own lives or in the American church. It happens only after we accept the necessary ending to the status quo rather than fight to perpetuate what is passing away. In each of our lives, communities, and contexts, the desert of the real will look different. But staying in Egypt won't do. That's not the good news of freedom, the liberation of the kingdom that God is always at work to establish on earth as it is in heaven.

But you know what else won't do? Staying in the wilderness—dying to the old season, to the old bondage, to the old ego and just staying dead. If we deconstruct our faith in Jesus—the Light!—to the point of demolition, being left with only cynicism, we lose. It's no way to live. If you are stuck halfway through a wilderness right now, you know this. You want something better. I wanted something better. Desperately.

We want resurrection.

We want abundant life.

We want belonging.

We want flourishing, finally.

And you know what? We are all undeserving of the gift of life in Jesus Christ. The sin within us and the brokenness around us are undeniable. Such a mess, right? But in his great love, God has shown all of us that we are yet worthy. The good life that Jesus offers is not just for other people. It's for you. *You* are the beloved of God.

Do you believe it?

Can you bring yourself to believe, right now, that the light is winning?

●   ●   ●

Once upon a time, my father gave me dog tags. He named me, and I believed him. Then he shamed me, and I believed him. And over time this calling that had been the center of my identity, that had helped me through so much, became a burden I could hardly bear. It was entangled in all manner of ego illusions, and when my great revealing came, truths about myself and my past were revealed. It was hard to believe that there was any hope to reclaim my calling. It seemed to lead only to pain, struggle, and devastation.

But it was necessary for my desire to please my father to end. It was necessary for my desire to follow in his footsteps, to be that powerful leader who is revered and significant, to die. Those were ego ambitions. And it took finally speaking the truth to myself and others, and cutting all ties with the dysfunction of the dividing, to realize this.

But what if I had stopped there? I probably would have given up. I'd have drowned in the death throes of my ego, become buried in the devastation of my shame and failure.

But that was not an option for me, and it's not an option for you either, because in our great pain, we have the opportunity to discover our deep loves, to open up a whole new kind of life, the depths of which we can hardly imagine. If we let go of who we've been trying to be and open up to who we really are, who we are meant to become, then our flourishing is just on the horizon. We just have to keep going—through the wilderness, through the desert of deconstruction, and into the promise on the other side. We just have to keep believing the light is winning.

I would be lying to you if I said that, after my own personal apocalypse, I have figured it all out and moved on with my life and it's better than ever, truly, you should try it! Because exiting the wilderness and starting this new beginning has been anything but easy or pain free. As Father Rohr said, it is a reality that is infinitely better and more spacious than anything that came before, yet it is simultaneously scary for that spaciousness. It is wonderfully and terribly *unknown.*

When I try to forecast the future, it just becomes overwhelming to consider. This expanse before me, these last days in the desert before whatever happens next—I just don't know, man! These are the times when I am more grateful than ever for my wife. She has a grasp on who and where we are, and a powerful internal compass for staying the course. I never stop learning from her leadership.

The one thing I know for sure is that we can't turn back, however tempting it might be to grab onto the old ego-shaped calling or perspective or way of life. Egypt might seem easier, but it's still bondage. Researcher and author Brene Brown says it best in her book *Rising Strong:* "During the process of rising we sometimes find ourselves homesick for a place that no longer exists. We want to go back to that moment before we walked into the arena. But there's nowhere to go back to."[1]

There's nowhere to go back to. I cannot fix the damage and disaster of an authoritarian upbringing, or resuscitate a ministry call from the first half of life, or pretend my theology and spirituality and politics have not progressed, or turn back the clock on relationships lost to toxicity, or make my life revolve around ministry obligations that no longer make a lick of sense. Because none of that even exists anymore. The eruptions of the real in my life have revealed all the unreality, all the illusion, tied up in those things. As Bonhoeffer described, I am graciously disillusioned now.

And in a very "meta" kind of way, it has taken the writing of this book to move me even farther down the road into this spaciousness. It has taken the changes that have happened inside of me while writing, and changes that have happened to my life on the outside during that same time. My little family has been on a wilderness sojourn since the traumatic end of our church plant, but through the wandering and searching, we find ourselves coming full circle, in a whole new way. We are ready to get back into the arena, to begin rising strong.

And that calling to serve Jesus and his church, the calling that was instilled in me at such a young age, confirmed by my fivefold ministry dog tags—can it ever be reclaimed? I know it can't be what it was, entangled in ego and shame, keeping me in bondage to empire business. It must be transformed. I must walk in my graduation. But I believe that as we put roots down into our new spiritual home, deep *religious* roots into a people and a place and a Methodist tradition, even this calling can be resurrected. Because beneath all the layers of struggle and disappointment, I know there is yet something real in that call. I've known it all along. I know that it is still part of who I am—not externally, not egotistically, but deeply and truly. I don't need or want the title of Apostle-Evangelist, or the significance or the following or the praise or the reputation. What I want is to join in God's mission and God's justice in the world, through the church, in the simplicity that grows out of the depths of everyday life and worship.

I believe I'm living out that calling to serve even as I write these words. Could the dog tags still, somehow, be pointing to something real? Well, apostolically, I'm writing so that we might all begin rebuilding, rebuilding the church and resurrecting religion, for the sake of the world. And, evangelistically, I'm writing so that we might all center on Jesus and place our hope in the Light, that we might live the abundant life, now and forever.

See? It's already happening. And it can happen for you too, no matter where you find yourself in this apocalyptic moment.

We are all, of course, called.

That's just the way the light-filled kingdom of God works.

The End Game

The apocalypse of the decline of faith in the US is an opportunity to repent and reform. It's an opportunity for Christians to own up to all of our empire business and embrace the Jesus-centered kingdom way. Our ideologies and illusions can't withstand this eruption of the real. And we will find flourishing only if we let go of all of them, all the ego-driven wish dreams that have held us in bondage.

But to do so will be painful. It will mean taking a loss—a loss of power, a loss of privilege, a loss of institutions, a loss of relevance, a loss of success. The things that so many fear about the decline of Christian faith in this country are the things required of us in this necessary suffering. The American church has been caught up for far too long in early stage religion. It is time to move on into maturity, into the second half of life.

And to those unwilling to face the great revealing, whose eyes are closed to the eruption of the real taking place all around us, who prefer to dismiss all of it and preserve the status quo, let me say this:

The thing about apocalypses is that they are uncontrollable. No amount of empire authority can rightly resist a kingdom revelation.

As your own eschatology likely teaches, such things come upon you like a thief in the night. And in the end, there's nothing you can do to stop it.

●　　　●　　　●

The apostle might as well have been prophesying over my life when he said:

But everything exposed by the light becomes visible—and everything that is illuminated becomes a light. This is why it is said:

> "Wake up, sleeper,
> rise from the dead,
> and Christ will shine on you."*

---

* Ephesians 5:13–14.

To believe the light is winning is to accept, to embrace even, the opportunity that our painful reality presents. It is to stop running from the light and instead let it expose us. Let it reveal who we really are, and who Jesus and his kingdom really are.

But believing the light is winning is also keeping the end game in view. Our waking up. Our rising strong. Not the same, but transformed and new. To true and deep and abundant life.

The very end game that John the Revelator describes in his Apocalypse:

> Then I saw "a new heaven and a new earth," for the first heaven and the first earth had passed away, and there was no longer any sea. I saw the Holy City, the new Jerusalem, coming down out of heaven from God, prepared as a bride beautifully dressed for her husband. And I heard a loud voice from the throne saying, "Look! God's dwelling place is now among the people, and he will dwell with them. They will be his people, and God himself will be with them and be their God. 'He will wipe every tear from their eyes. There will be no more death' or mourning or crying or pain, for the old order of things has passed away."
>
> He who was seated on the throne said, "I am making everything new!"*

Yes, this promise of ultimate restoration—where heaven and earth are made fully new—is yet future, the ultimate healing of all the world's sin and brokenness. This is the last new beginning, after the final necessary ending.

---

* Revelation 21:1–5.

But it is this ultimate not-yet that comes rushing into the now through the Christian life of death and resurrection. That's the life we're living, the life the church in the US is living too, one caught up in the same Jesus-shaped pattern. We find ourselves on the verge of "everything new," where the death that must come to all our ego and empire business gives way to the good, abundant life.

The pain doesn't last forever, nor the suffering. And when it comes, we may be able to see it for what it is: the sign that resurrection is surely on the way. I can almost feel Jesus wiping away the tears. Maybe you can too.

John continues:

> And he carried me away in the Spirit to a mountain great and high, and showed me the Holy City, Jerusalem, coming down out of heaven from God . . . I did not see a temple in the city, because the Lord God Almighty and the Lamb are its temple. The city does not need the sun or the moon to shine on it, for the glory of God gives it light, and the Lamb is its lamp. The nations will walk by its light, and the kings of the earth will bring their splendor into it. On no day will its gates ever be shut, for there will be no night there. The glory and honor of the nations will be brought into it.*

What a glorious vision! But maybe we've been too quick to dismiss this imagery as ethereal and fantastic. Of course, it's describing an ultimate reality, but what if we patterned our understanding of the church based on this great revealing from John?

---

* Revelation 21:10, 22–26.

Think of it—in this ultimate new beginning, there is no temple. No temple at all! For the Father and the Son—the Lamb—*are* the temple. John's point here is not to disregard religious ritual in the temple (or the church) now but rather to show that when all is said and done, the ultimate reason for the church's existence will be present fully in bodily form. That ultimate reason is Jesus himself! So can there be any doubt that a church that isn't centered on Jesus, absorbed in the rooted religious and Spirit-filled worship of the King, is really no church at all? If we deconstruct even the center of our worship and the passionate practices through which heaven meets earth, then we lose any substance and become an empty shell. A zombie religion.

But the vision doesn't stop there. There's also no need for the sun or the moon because the New Jerusalem is lit by the glory of God, and "the Lamb is its lamp." Jesus—the Light!—shines throughout the new city, with sunlike brilliance. And the light will continually draw all people to the new city, to the kingdom of God. The light will always be winning.

And there, right at the end, is an incredible promise that is also meant to guide the church throughout all time, and especially in this apocalyptic time: "its gates will never shut."

The new city faces out. The new city includes all. The new city is there for "the nations," for the mission of God and the justice of God and the kingdom of God outside the lines.

If the Christian faith in the US is going to move into this new beginning, it must stop existing for itself and start existing for the sake of the world.

It must stop shutting its gates.

●　　●　　●

Author Glennon Doyle Melton says this thing about pain and love and being brave, and it rings true for me. Maybe it will for you too. She says, "I've never let myself trust love because I've never let myself trust pain. What if pain—like love—is just a place brave people visit?"[2]

Then she adds, "The bravest people I know are those who've walked through the fire and come out the other side. They are those who've overcome, not those who've had nothing to overcome."[3]

It reminds me of this famous verse in John's Apocalypse, from the King James Version we used to read in that Texas cult: "Now is come salvation, and strength, and the kingdom of our God, and the power of his Christ: for the accuser of our brethren is cast down, which accused them before our God day and night. And they overcame him by the blood of the Lamb, and by the word of their testimony; and they loved not their lives unto the death."[*]

Now is come salvation—to you! And strength—to you! And the kingdom—to you! And the power—to you!

Because anyone or anything (including yourself) that is accusing you, that has sought to destroy you, that thought it could end you is cast down.

And *you* have overcome. You know how? By centering your whole life on Jesus, the Lamb. And by owning and speaking the word of your testimony, your story.

You are an overcomer. You are one of the brave ones! You have faced the pain and trusted what it would reveal. You have willingly walked through the illuminating fire instead of running from it. You have faced down your apocalyptic moment. And now

---

[*] Revelation 12:10–11.

you know, like never before, that you are the beloved of God, and you are called to a good faith and a good life of flourishing.

In our sin and in the brokenness of our lives, we are forever undeserving of the gift of life in Christ Jesus. But he has declared us worthy by unconditionally loving us. And knowing this, we may now begin to live up to that great love.

Everything—and everyone—that is illuminated *becomes* a light.

This is our calling.

Thanks be to God.

Notes

Chapter 1: Apocalypse Now

1. "America's Changing Religious Landscape," Pew Research Center, May 12, 2015, http://www.pewforum.org/2015/05/12/ americas-changing-religious-landscape/.

2. Michael Lipka, "Five Key Findings about the Changing U.S. Religious Landscape," Pew Research Center, May 12, 2015, http:// www.pewresearch.org/fact-tank/2015/05/12/5-key-findings-u-s -religious-landscape/.

3. Bradley Wright, "The Rise of the Unaffiliated—The Religious Nones," *Black, White, and Gray*, February 28, 2013, http://www .patheos.com/blogs/blackwhiteandgray/2013/02/the-rise-of-the -unaffiliated-the-religious-nones/.

4. Becka A. Alper, "Millennials Are Less Religious Than Older Americans, but Just as Spiritual," Pew Research Center, November 23, 2015, http://www.pewresearch.org/fact-tank/2015/ 11/23/millennials-are-less-religious-than-older-americans-but-just -as-spiritual/.

5. Lipka, "Five Key Findings."

6. Jonathan Merritt, "Evangelicals' Claims of Conservative Supremacy Are Overstated—and Misread America's Religious Landscape," Religion News Service, May 13, 2015, http:// jonathanmerritt.religionnews.com/2015/05/13/evangelicals-claims -of-conservative-supremacy-are-overstated-and-misread-americas -religious-landscape/.

7. Jon Meacham, "Meacham: The End of Christian America," *Newsweek*, April 3, 2009, http://www.newsweek.com/meacham -end-christian-america-77125.

8. Steve McAlpine, "Stage Two Exile: Are You Ready for It?" Gospel Coalition Australia, June 1, 2015, https://australia.the gospelcoalition.org/article/stage-two-exile-are-you-ready-for-it.

9. Michael Spencer, "The Coming Evangelical Collapse," *Christian Science Monitor*, March 10, 2009, http://www.csmonitor.com/ Commentary/Opinion/2009/0310/p09s01-coop.html.

10. Michael J. Gorman, *Reading Revelation Responsibly: Uncivil Worship and Witness; Following the Lamb into the New Creation* (Eugene, Ore.: Cascade Books, 2011), Kindle location 58.

11. Ibid., 456–57.

12. *Apocalypse Now*, directed by Francis Ford Coppola, performances by Martin Sheen, Marlon Brando, Robert Duvall (United Artists, 1979).

Chapter 2: Beyond the Numbers

1. David E. Fitch, *The End of Evangelicalism? Discerning a New Faithfulness for Mission* (Eugene, Ore.: Cascade Books, 2011), 24. Used by permission of Wipf and Stock Publishers.

2. Ibid., 27.

3. Ibid., 28.

4. I am indebted to Pastor Brian Zahnd for the concept of breaking good versus breaking bad and its connection to control. See his excellent sermon at Word of Life Church on September 29, 2013, http://wolc.com/podcast/breaking-bad/.

5. "Buyout," *Breaking Bad*, written by Vince Gilligan and Gennifer Hutchison, directed by Colin Bucksey, Sony Pictures Television in association with American Movie Classics (AMC), 2012.

6. John's telling of this story adds the detail that Judas was the objector and that his motive was not really helping the poor but skimming a little off the top for himself (John 12:6). I agree with most commentators who take Mark's version at face value.

7. Brian Zahnd, "The Book of Revelation," personal blog, 2015, http://brianzahnd.com/2015/09/the-book-of-revelation/.

8. Sarah Pulliam Bailey, "Evangelical Sex Abuse Record 'Worse' Than Catholic, Says Billy Graham's Grandson Boz Tchividijian," *Huffington Post*, October 1, 2013, http://www.huffingtonpost.com/2013/10/01/protestant-sex-abuse-boz-tchividijian_n_4019347.html.

Chapter 3: A Problem with Authority

1. Josh Packard and Ashleigh Hope, *Church Refugees: Sociologists Reveal Why People Are Done with Church but Not Their Faith* (Denver: Group, 2015), 21, 23.

2. Ibid., 21, 23.

3. Josh Packard, personal interview, May 10, 2016. Used with permission.

4. Packard and Hope, *Church Refugees*, 57.

5. Ibid., 72.

6. Cathy Lynn Grossman, "Meet the 'Nominals' Who Are Drifting from Judaism and Christianity," Religion News Service, October 1, 2013, http://religionnews.com/2013/10/01/meet -nominals-drifting-judaism-christianity/.

7. Packard, personal interview, May 10, 2016.

Chapter 4: American Empire

1. I'm indebted to Dr. Grant R. Osborne for this background on Laodicea. See *Life Application Bible Commentary: Revelation* (Carol Stream, Ill.: Tyndale, 2000), 46–48.

2. Michael J. Gorman, *Reading Revelation Responsibly: Uncivil Worship and Witness; Following the Lamb into the New Creation* (Eugene, Ore.: Cascade Books, 2011), 96. Used by permission of Wipf and Stock Publishers.

3. Ibid.

4. Matthew Paul Turner, "The Different Meanings of End of Days," National Geographic Channel, 2016, http://channel.national

geographic.com/the-story-of-god-with-morgan-freeman/articles/
the-different-meanings-of-end-of-days/.

5. Ibid.

6. Sarah Pulliam Bailey, "Jerry Falwell Jr.: 'If More Good People Had Concealed-Carry Permits, Then We Could End Those' Islamist Terrorists," *Washington Post*, December 5, 2015, https://www .washingtonpost.com/news/acts-of-faith/wp/2015/12/05/liberty -university-president-if-more-good-people-had-concealed-guns-we -could-end-those-muslims/.

7. Eugene Peterson, *Reversed Thunder* (San Francisco: HarperCollins, 1991), 77.

8. Brian Zahnd, "War of the Lamb," blog, May 8, 2016, http://brian zahnd.com/2016/05/war-of-the-lamb.

Chapter 6: Roll Credits (On the First Half of Life)

1. Richard Rohr, *Falling Upward: A Spirituality for the Two Halves of Life* (San Francisco: Wiley, 2011), xvi.

2. Ibid., 339.

3. Ibid., 221, 270.

4. Richard Rohr, "Changing Our Minds," Center for Action and Contemplation, March 29, 2016, https://cac.org/changing-our -minds-2016-03-29/.

5. Ibid.

6. N. T. Wright, *Paul for Everyone: The Prison Letters* (Louisville: Westminster John Knox, 2004), 48.

Chapter 7: The Desert of Deconstruction

1. *The Matrix*, directed by the Wachowski Brothers, performances by Keanu Reeves, Laurence Fishburne, Carrie-Anne Moss (Warner Brothers, 1999).

2. Jean Baudrillard, *Simulacra and Simulation* (Ann Arbor, Mich.: University of Michigan Press, 1994). Quote taken from https:// en.wikipedia.org/wiki/Welcome_to_the_Desert_of_the_Real.

3. Richard Rohr, *Falling Upward: A Spirituality for the Two Halves of Life* (San Francisco: Wiley, 2011), Kindle location 368.

4. Pope Francis, *Evangelii Gaudium* (Vatican Press, 2013), http://w2 .vatican.va/content/francesco/en/apost_exhortations/documents/ papa-francesco_esortazione-ap_20131124_evangelii-gaudium .html.

5. Garrison Keillor, "Bob McDonnell and the Rolex Christians," *Washington Post*, May 5, 2016, https://www.washingtonpost.com/ opinions/bob-mcdonnell-and-the-rolex-christians/2016/05/05/735 ca968-1247-11e6-81b4-581a5c4c42df_story.html.

Chapter 8: Exit through the Wilderness

1. Jonathan Martin, *How to Survive a Shipwreck* (Grand Rapids: Zondervan, 2016), 138–39. Used by permission of Zondervan.

2. Tim Suttle, "Favorite Stanley Hauerwas Quotes," *Paperback Theology*, October 3, 2014, http://www.patheos.com/blogs/paper backtheology/2014/10/favorite-stanley-hauerwas-quotes.html.

3. Rachel Held Evans, *Searching for Sunday* (Nashville: Thomas Nelson, 2015), 225. Used by permission of Thomas Nelson.

4. Richard Rohr, *Falling Upward: A Spirituality for the Two Halves of Life* (San Francisco: Wiley, 2011), 85.

5. Shane Blackshear, "Seminary Dropout 91: Rob Bell, from the Everything Is Spiritual Tour," *Seminary Dropout*, podcast, July 16, 2015, http://shaneblackshear.com/robbell.

Chapter 9: Songs of the Resurrected and the Undead

1. John Wesley, "Thoughts Upon Methodism," IMARC, 1999, http://www.imarc.cc/one_meth/vol-02-no-02.html.

Chapter 10: Making Progress

1. Emily L. Stephens, "True Detective: 'Church in Ruins,'" *A.V. Club*, July 27, 2015, http://www.avclub.com/tvclub/true-detective -church-ruins-222873.

2. "Form and Void," *True Detective*, written by Nic Pizzolatto, directed by Cary Joji Fukunaga (Home Box Office, 2014).
3. David Kinnaman and Gabe Lyons, *UnChristian* (Grand Rapids: Baker, 2007), 182, 184.
4. Gabe Lyons, *The Next Christians* (New York: Random House, 2010), 30.
5. David Kinnaman and Gabe Lyons, *Good Faith* (Grand Rapids: Baker, 2016), 21. Used with permission.
6. Ibid.
7. Ibid., 13–14.
8. Ibid., 72.
9. Ibid., 232.
10. N. T. Wright, "Look at Jesus," *Work of the People*, n.d., http://www.theworkofthepeople.com/look-at-jesus.

Chapter 11: Resurrected Religion

1. Miroslav Volf, *Flourishing* (New Haven: Yale University Press, 2015), ix.
2. Ibid.
3. Ibid., 22.
4. Brian Zahnd, *Water to Wine* (St. Joseph: Spello Press, 2016), 68–69.
5. Nathan Decker, "The Great Thanksgiving for World Communion Sunday," Discipleship Ministries, http://www.umcdiscipleship.org/resources/the-great-thanksgiving-for-world-communion-sunday. Adapted from A Service of Word and Table I & II ©1972, 1980, 1985, 1989 The United Methodist Publishing House. Used by permission.
6. John Wesley, "The Duty of Constant Communion," Sermon 101 (1872), http://www.umcmission.org/Find-Resources/John-Wesley-Sermons/Sermon-101-The-Duty-of-Constant-Communion.
7. Zahnd, *Water to Wine*, 80–89.

Chapter 12: Post-Apocalyptic Christianity

1. See Ben Witherington III, *The Acts of the Apostles: A Socio-Rhetorical Commentary* (Grand Rapids: Eerdmans, 1998), 132.
2. Dietrich Bonhoeffer, *Life Together* (New York: Harper and Row, 1954), 27.
3. Richard Rohr, *Falling Upward: A Spirituality for the Two Halves of Life* (San Francisco: Wiley, 2011), 81.
4. Alan J. Roxburgh, *Structured for Mission* (Downer's Grove, Ill.: InterVarsity, 2015), 133.
5. RethinkChurch, website banner, http://rethinkchurch.org.
6. Walter Brueggemann, Faith and Culture Conference, "The Prophetic Imagination," Word of Life Church, St. Joseph, Mo., 2015, http://www.wolc.com/conferenceaudio/.
7. Stanley Hauerwas and William H. Willimon, *The Holy Spirit* (Nashville: Abingdon, 2015), 6–7. Copyright ©2015 by The United Methodist Publishing House. Used by permission. All rights reserved.
8. Ibid., 50–51.
9. N. T. Wright, "Paul and Caesar: A New Reading of Romans," NTWrightPage, n.d., http://ntwrightpage.com/Wright_Paul_Caesar_Romans.htm.
10. N. T. Wright, *How God Became King: The Forgotten Story of the Gospels* (New York: HarperOne, 2012), 140.
11. Joel B. Green, *The Gospel of Luke* (Grand Rapids: Eerdmans, 1997), 540–41.
12. Walter Brueggemann, Faith and Culture Conference, "Out of Babylon," Word of Life Church, St. Joseph, Mo., 2015, http://www.wolc.com/conferenceaudio/.
13. Ibid.
14. Erik Sherman, "America Is the Richest, and Most Unequal, Country," *Fortune*, September 30, 2015, http://fortune.com/2015/09/30/america-wealth-inequality/.
15. Elizabeth Stoker Bruenig, "Johns Hopkins Talk—Christianity, Poverty, Welfare," personal blog, April 27, 2016, http://

elizabethstokerbruenig.com/2016/04/27/johns-hopkins-talk
-christianity-poverty-welfare/.

16. "Criminal Justice Fact Sheet," NAACP, n.d., http://www.naacp
.org/pages/criminal-justice-fact-sheet.

17. Michelle Alexander, *The New Jim Crow* (New York: The New
Press, 2010), 7.

18. Ta-Nehisi Coates, "The Case for Reparations," *The Atlantic*, June
2014, http://www.theatlantic.com/magazine/archive/2014/06/the
-case-for-reparations/361631/.

19. Bruenig, "Johns Hopkins Talk."

Chapter 13: The Light Is Winning

1. Brene Brown, *Rising Strong* (New York: Spiegel and Grau, 2015), 5.

2. Glennon Doyle Melton, *Love Warrior* (New York: Flatiron Books,
2016), 201.

3. Ibid., 204.